*The Quick and Easy
Vegetarian Cookbook*

The Quick and Easy Vegetarian Cookbook

RUTH ANN MANNERS
AND WILLIAM MANNERS

M. Evans and Company, Inc. | New York, N.Y. 10017

Library of Congress Cataloging in Publication Data

Manners, Ruth Ann.
    The quick and easy vegetarian cookbook.

    Includes index.
    1. Vegetarian cookery. I. Manners, William,
1907–   joint author. II. Title.
TX837.M294   641.5'636   78-2259
ISBN 0-87131-260-3 Hardcover
ISBN 0-87131-303-0 Paperback

Design by Al Cetta
Manufactured in the United States of America
9 8

For Tracy, Tim, Jane, Julie, Michael, Jonathan and Paul

We acknowledge with thanks the support, advice and encouragement of the following: Georgia Bauer, Dot Cole, Barbara Fazio, Adele Gabowitz, Ethel Gorham, Marguerite Gustafson, Anne Harris, Alan Harvey, Mary Ellen and Guy Henle, Ginger Kersjes, Florence and George Klumb, Regina Koppel, Debby and Jay Levinson, Mary and Rod Lopez-Fabrega, Paul Manners, Linda Miklos, Roberta Pryor, Fay Rosenberg, Harriet Salerno, R. A. Seelig, Allyn Seidman, Nancy Sweet and Pamela Veley, Inge Maerowitz, Robin Polley and Cathy Wolff.

Also, special thanks to Jane and Tim for their help in typing the manuscript; to Frank Ford, author of *The Simpler Life Cookbook*; to Dr. Louis B. Rockland of the United States Department of Agriculture, and to all those who tasted our recipes in the process of development.

Contents

Introduction

When a friend learned we were writing a vegetarian cookbook, she reacted by writing to us immediately: "Too bad to be so lazy, but for a noncook like me a cholesterolic hamburger will always be easier to prepare—or even to eat raw—than anything needing chopping, slicing, blending, mixing. . . ."

Her statement can be regarded as a *Summation of People Versus Vegetarian Cookery*. Therefore, we feel that our book may well perform a public service if it helps make the vegetarian cuisine quick and easy. By being quick and easy, this cuisine may also help do away with the desperate need felt by many people for packaged convenience foods, with their chemicals and high prices. Confirmed vegetarians may very well profit in a special way. We hope our recipes will make it possible for them to enjoy dishes they've desired with gourmet passion, but feared to tackle because of their complexity and long preparation time.

Still, we realize it's natural to be leery of shortcut cooking. It calls to mind fast-food franchises, stamped-out meals, and instant soups straight from the lab. It does not follow, however, that long-in-preparation time is essential to excellence. (A restaurant in New York, specializing in soups, has a sign proclaiming its lentil soup is four and a half hours in the making, implying that this makes their soup beyond compare.) The proof of the pudding continues to be in the eating, not in the length of time required to prepare it. Testing our recipes therefore included tasting the finished products.

Sound nutrition also entered into our creation of recipes. We have avoided the use of refined ingredients, or ingredients that are nutritionally suspect. We have also specified fresh fruits and vegetables whenever possible. Our soups do not consist of a canned soup camouflaged with noncanned embellishments.

We felt that our recipes should not only contribute to health—and this included minimizing the energy that the cook expended—but to conservation of fuel as well. There's no reason, for example, why

12

foods cannot continue baking after the oven has been turned off. All that this change in procedure requires is some precise calculations. If a dish calls for 30 minutes of baking at 400°, the oven might be turned off after 20 minutes and the dish remain in the oven while it cools for 15 or 20 minutes. (The fuel conservation ideal: to put food to be baked in a cold oven and to take it out, completely done, from a cold oven.) Top-of-range dishes are also fuel savers, as is undercooking rather than overcooking, and using a pressure cooker whenever possible.

Certain terms require definition. What is quick? What is easy? Obviously, if an entrée is prepared in five minutes, it is quick. But is it still quick if it takes three times that long? The answer is yes, when "three times that long" is still comparatively fast. For example, eggplant parmigiana usually takes a half hour to prepare; if it can be done in half that time, we think it deserves to be regarded as quick. And we shall declare an entrée quick and easy, even though it requires considerable cooking or baking time after it has been quickly and easily prepared.

"Easy" is also determined by comparison. Recipes that eliminate preparation steps—and simplify, in every possible way—are obviously easier recipes. When a recipe is easy, you know without question that it is, just as you know when one is difficult. It should also be noted that the time we've specified as needed for the preparation of a particular recipe is merely an approximation. Don't let it make you rush madly around the kitchen, or feel inferior if you can't complete a recipe in the time stated.

In spite of these assurances, the book's recipes may still evoke an athletic event with stopwatch in hand and records to be made. Our intention is far different; we simply want to offer a wholesome, delicious cuisine that's easily achieved.

The recipes are presented as they are, for the sake of simplicity, clarity and convenience. In many cookbooks, recipes start with a list of all the ingredients required, followed by directions as to their use. To minimize the time it takes to find the ingredients referred to, we have not separated them from the directions. Instead, we have set them in boldface and put them directly ahead of the directions that apply to them. Thus as you move along in a recipe, you will be able to tell more easily what ingredients are needed and how they are to be used.

We hope this book will be especially helpful to the following:

Those who are always on the lookout for new meatless recipes, whether easy or hard.

Those who spend the day at work and have little time for cooking.

College students who have neither the time nor money for complicated dishes, but have a ravenous passion for food.

Those who want to save money.

Those who believe vegetarian cooking is too difficult or too dull.

Those interested in health and natural foods.

Those who want an occasional dietary change.

The vegetarian hiker, camper, or boatowner whose cooking facilities are limited, and who wants to relax while on vacation but still not subsist on canned beans or their equivalent.

Nonvegetarians who have a vegetarian child or two and have to prepare two menus.

Nonvegetarians who have vegetarian friends they would like to entertain.

And, finally, we hope this book will help the avid gardener who finds himself with a bumper crop on his hands and needs easy ways to use his produce.

Timesaving Approaches

Wonderful though timesaving mechanical aids may be, the human element—when understood and exploited—can help in getting things done in the kitchen. The right approach springs from a well-known command: "If you can't stand the heat, get out of the kitchen!" And there can be all manner of heat—all kinds of pressures: the bread's not rising; why has the cake fallen?; the company will arrive any minute now and I'm not dressed and I have the salad to do and the kitchen looks like a disaster area and . . . and . . . and. . . .

There *are* answers.

1. Ignore the rationalization that one saves time by not keeping an orderly kitchen as one goes along. Ignore it, because it's false. A disorderly kitchen causes you to waste time. It trips you up physically, makes you wretched mentally. We know a role model for all nonprofessionals, a short-order cook who, besieged by what seems an impossible number of orders, manages to remain unflustered. All his motions are smooth, quick, effortless—and include wiping the counter whenever it needs it, putting away dishes, and keeping pots and pans in their place.

2. Be sure you have all the ingredients you need for a recipe before you start. For example, it's frustrating and a waste of time to grease bread pans and measure flour for a bread baking, only to discover that you're out of yeast.

3. When a dinner party looms, you'll be serene if you've planned and prepared ahead, lightening the burden by doing a little over several days, instead of trying to do everything at once.

4. Know a recipe thoroughly before you start. Just reading it over a few times isn't enough, for you'll still have to refer to it again and again. Time will actually be saved if you memorize the recipe. This will also give you the feeling of power that a creator enjoys; creators, after all, don't have to refer to the work of others.

If you insist, perhaps with a tinge of boasting, that you have a poor memory, all is not lost. Your goal can be reached in a number of ways. Make a chart for each of your favorite recipes—ingredients and directions should be in large block letters, a special boon to those who use reading glasses. All you need to do, as you work, is look up and easily spot what you have to do next. The same results can be achieved by covering the inside of a kitchen cabinet door with a blackboard on which you print the recipe *du jour*. If you're electronically inclined, you might tape recipes. Record them slowly and with long pauses, so that when you prepare a dish you'll be able to keep up with the step-by-step instructions.

5. We have found that one can do a recipe much more quickly and easily by doing it a number of successive times. Familiarity, in this instance, breeds assurance. But you may meet with a degree of hostility from those who find themselves, in their words, "always eating the same old thing." To avoid this emotional situation, simply alter the oft-repeated recipe just a bit. For example, the appearance and flavor of the bread you've been making regularly can be changed merely by using a different sweetener. There are many to choose from: brown sugar, honey, blackstrap molasses, a combination of honey and blackstrap molasses, dried fruits. . . .

6. Memorize basic measurements. This will make it unnecessary for you to look them up each and every time-wasting time. For example, it's helpful to know that there are 3 teaspoons in 1 tablespoon. When a recipe calls for 4 teaspoons, you'll be able to take care of that with 1 tablespoon and 1 teaspoon instead of laboriously measuring out 4 individual teaspoons. Or if you can't find your ¼-cup measure, or it needs washing, it's handy to know that 4 tablespoons equal ¼ cup. Sticks of butter usually don't tell you that there are 5⅓ tablespoons in a third of a cup, and recipes are forever—or so it seems—calling for ⅓ cup butter. Therefore, you obviously save time by learning that fact once and for all.

7. Always have the tools you need readily available. Measuring spoons have the habit of straying, and it's a good idea to have so many that you never need to look for one. Have an abundance of measuring cups, too. Though they can't hide themselves as readily as measuring spoons, they're so often dirty just when needed that it seems eerily more than coincidence.

Essential kitchen aids should always be of the best—and in good shape. Knives sharp. The measurements on glass measuring cups not eroded to unreadability.

The accessibility of items in the refrigerator is also vital. This is made possible by your orderly mind—orderly in the kitchen if not elsewhere. It always sees to it that a particular item is invariably on the same shelf and at the same spot on that shelf. This eliminates a great deal of time spent in frantic search. It also helps to store food in transparent containers, so that you don't find yourself struggling with the tight-fitting lid of an opaque container only to discover it doesn't have what you want.

8. Another dictum for the orderly mind: To avoid the time-consuming quandary of not remembering whether you've put a certain ingredient in the mixing bowl, always use ingredients in the order in which they're presented in a recipe.

9. Remember—from brutal experience—that you can only do a limited amount in a brief period. Plan a meal accordingly. Even when using quick and easy recipes, it's an error to attempt to prepare seven courses in a half hour. That's strictly for fantasy.

Timesaving Equipment

Finely chopped, thinly sliced, grated, ground, and *minced* are key words in vegetarian recipes. They are also probably the reason why vegetarian cooking has a reputation for taking too much time, too much work, and too much bother.

Is the reputation deserved? Certainly.

Is the reputation necessary? Absolutely not!

There are huge, gaping loopholes through which you can avoid all the drudgery and dog work in vegetarian cooking!

But, first, why all the slicing, chopping, and grating? There are good reasons for it. Orientals have known for centuries that reducing food to small bits before cooking . . .

- Enhances the flavor by blending textures.
- Increases eye appeal by preserving bright, fresh colors.
- Saves fuel cost by greatly shortening cooking time.

What the Chinese and Japanese may not have realized, as they quickly tossed and cooked their food by the stir-fry method, was that they were also preserving its nutritive value. Perhaps all these benefits were more important to them than saving time and work.

Today, thousands of years later, we still want to enjoy all these benefits, and also save time and work. And we can. . . .

So now for the loopholes! Simply put, they are the excellent mechanical devices that do all your chopping, slicing, and grating for you—and a few other things besides.

Obviously, much of the chopping and cutting can be done with a set of good sharp knives. With considerable practice, you may even become as adept as an hibachi chef. But if time is money, and the kitchen is not the place to spend it, then consider the following helpers.

We are not suggesting that you must have them all (you'd probably soon run out of storage space or money, or both), but these tools and equipment win our vote. Some of them may seem expensive, but one small machine can often take the place of a whole kitchen clutter of small gadgets and, in the end, cost no more.

The heavy-duty food preparer.

Most people call it a mixer, but it's much more than that. It can be the genie of your kitchen if you get one that has the sinew and muscle to do everything you command. Certainly, it must be big, heavy, powerful, and versatile.

Our own personal genie is the KitchenAid Model K-45. It's a home version of a commercially used machine. The mass-produced, competitively priced mixers that most people buy just don't compare. It seems expensive, yes. It is. But you'll get so much more use and pleasure out of it, you won't regret its price. If you buy a lighter-duty model, you may be sorry. You just won't be able to use it for as many things, or as often.

The paraprofessional heavy-duty machine we're talking about does everything. It has a flat beater for cakes, pastry, mashed potatoes, etc. It has a wire whip for eggs, mayonnaise, milk drinks, etc. It has a dough hook for kneading yeast breads.

With attachments, it's also a juice extractor, colander and sieve, food grinder, slicer and shredder, ice-cream freezer, can opener, and even a grain mill. The grain mill attachment is a special gem. By making it possible to grind whole grains as needed, it eliminates the necessity to refrigerate whole grain flours to prevent their becoming rancid. You can buy whole grains in quantity and grind them as the occasion arises. You can also create your own special combinations and blends.

Almost any day, you'll find our machine at work kneading bread, mixing up a batch of cookies, making coleslaw, or grating Parmesan cheese. And more, more, more.

The KitchenAid K-45 is a rather large machine that may cause space problems in a tiny kitchen. Ideally, it should be kept at the ready on the counter, with its attachments in a drawer nearby, so that you can call upon it without ado. If you have to drag it out of . storage each time it's used, you may be disinclined to make the most of it, and it's a beautiful, valuable genie.

The food processor.

This little miracle worker originated in France as a large, commercial-sized processor designed for restaurant use. Then someone had the bright idea of making a smaller version for the home kitchen, and the Cuisinart® Food Processor was born. This small machine is rarely seen in French home kitchens, but when imported to this country, it caught on immediately, and revolutionized food preparation from Maine to California.

What can it do for you? It can slice, grate, mince, shred, and purée the daylights out of any kind of food you might care to feed it. All those tedious jobs that used to slow you down can be performed in seconds. You must be careful, or you'll overdo it. Indeed, there's a temptation, especially at first, to become mesmerized by the efficiency of this dazzling tool and reduce everything to a sublime, satin smoothness. You know what *that* can do to your gums!

In addition to the swift slicing and chopping action, the food processor can produce flaky piecrust, perfect mayonnaise, mix and knead bread doughs, make smooth nut butters, blend salad dressings, turn frozen fruit into instant sherbet, make dry cottage cheese into a low-calorie cream cheese substitute, and much more.

Naturally, the great success of the Cuisinart has spawned a flood of imitations. Most of them are less expensive, but not all of them are as good as the original. Compare. Watch demonstrations and, if possible, try them out for yourself. If you decide to buy a food processor, you'll probably soon wonder how you got along without it.

The blender.

The blender has been around for a long time. When Waring first introduced it, it created much the same kind of excitement as the Cuisinart food processor. It's a great little machine and can do many of the things that a food processor does, but on a smaller scale. Instead of doing a batch in a single operation, it may be necessary to divide ingredients into smaller portions and complete the processing in several loads. Besides being slower than a processor, its results, in some cases, are of somewhat lesser quality. There are some processing tasks it simply cannot handle.

Food processor owners, however, are not likely to discard their blenders. There are some things a blender can do that a food processor can't. It has something to do with the size and shape of the two containers. The two appliances can be used in tandem—doing part of a recipe in one and part in the other. You can even make it a "ménage à trois" and bring the KitchenAid food preparer into the act. This combination certainly speeds things up.

Blenders take little space, are easily moved from one place to another, and are not outrageously expensive. They are a special boon to the student living in a dormitory, and to the apartment dweller with a miniscule kitchen.

Newer models have refinements such as timers, on-and-off pulsating action, removable blade assembly for easy cleaning, relay-controlled speeds, solid-state circuitry, automatic turnoff in case of a power failure, and 5-cup containers. Of these, we consider the removable blade assembly and 5-cup container to be the most noteworthy.

In buying a blender, you'll be wise to invest in one of the better models of a well-known manufacturer. You may find that it has fewer push buttons and gadgetry. After all, who needs such an infinite variety of speeds? With no more than eight push buttons, their larger size and more convenient spacing make the machine easier to use and clean.

Additional Helpers and Timesavers

Pressure cooker.

We feel that your cooking will be quicker and easier if you have a pressure cooker—aluminum or stainless steel, four quart or six. It does a superbly swift job of cooking such refractory vegetables as winter squash and beets. As our recipes will show, it's also marvelous for preparing soups and vegetable stews.

There are a couple of drawbacks, however. Since you can't see what's going on in a pressure cooker—and can't easily lift the lid to check—it's easy to overcook foods. Be on the alert. Watch the time carefully. And to cook vegetables more amenable than those mentioned above, that reach the point of crisp tenderness in approximately 7 minutes, you might as well use a collapsible steamer basket instead. The other drawback is the fear some people have of pressure cookers. They do hiss occasionally, but the hiss is no more harmful than a pussycat's.

The six quart pressure cooker, we feel, is the most useful size.

Juicer.

An attachment for reaming juice from oranges, lemons, limes, and grapefruit is available for some heavy-duty mixers and food processors. You'll also find that there are several small electric juicing machines on the market that are quite good. No matter what the type, an electric juicer will save you time. It will also provide you with better-tasting juices than the frozen concentrates.

Electric knife.

What we like best about our electric knife is the way it slices bread. Even bread that's oven-fresh can be neatly sliced to any thickness, and loaves with thick, crisp crusts—as hard as armor—

don't end up mangled and squashed. The electric knife can also be used to slice cheeses, vegetables, and frozen foods.

Collapsible vegetable steamer.

This handy little basket is made of stainless steel and can adjust to fit nearly any pan. It stands on three legs to keep the food to be steamed out of the water, and has a small, lifting handle in the center.

Knives.

Since we're interested in saving you time and work, we recommend stainless steel knives rather than the carbon blades touted for so long by the "experts" as the better choice. The stainless steel knives that are being made now are as good as any carbon blade in sharpening to a fine edge and maintaining that edge. They're also much easier to keep clean and don't stain or discolor.

Our advice: buy the best knives you can afford—a few good ones, even though they seem horribly expensive, rather than many "bargains." A cheap knife, you'll find, may not cut just when you want it to. Nothing's more frustrating than that—and time consuming. A dull knife can also be dangerous.

Slicers, graters, and choppers.

If you haven't been blessed with power slicing and grating equipment, you should consider several manual devices that can do an excellent job of cutting food into small bits.

We've found the four-sided, stainless steel grater-slicer that sits squarely on the counter, and which one holds steady by a handle at the top, to be more satisfactory and safe than the single-sided type that must be held at an angle or laid flat across the bowl.

The mandoline cutter is a first-rate slicing tool. It rests at an angle on the counter and can be adjusted to vary the thickness of slices.

A table model rotary slicer and shredder, with interchangeable cones for various functions similar to those that are available for the KitchenAid mixer, is simple to use and easy to clean.

Mouli graters, imported from France, may appear inconsequential. They do have virtues, however. For one thing, they're very handy for grating small amounts of cheese or nuts. Another very real convenience is that you can grate directly into the cooking pot or over the top of a casserole.

One of our favorite small gadgets is a tiny nutmeg grater. It hangs on a hook in clear view. It has a small compartment which holds one nutmeg—ready to be grated. No need to get out the nutmeg jar and round up a grater. It's all right there!

A Swiss-made food chopper, with rotating blade and plunger action, chops vegetables, nuts, and cheese reasonably fast. If you're getting a chopper of this kind, be sure to get a good one. We say this because there are many flimsily-made, worthless versions.

The chef's knife should also be your knife for general chopping and mincing. It comes in different lengths and has a triangular blade. All you do is put its point on the chopping block. Then, with a downward, rhythmic movement, do your chopping and mincing. All it takes is a little practice—very little, really.

Two-handled rocker knives are excellent for chopping mushrooms and herbs. Perhaps you'd prefer the professional model rocker that has three blades.

And here is a list—in alphabetical order—of other small helpers that we feel should be in the well-equipped kitchen:

biscuit cutter
cookbook holder (transparent plastic)
colander
food mill
garlic press
grapefruit knife
kitchen shears
melon baller
pastry brush
pastry cloth and knit rolling pin cover
strainer
spinning salad-dryer basket
swivel potato peeler
thermometer (yeast, candy)
timer
tongs
vegetable brush
wire whisks (several sizes)
wooden spoons (large ones for mixing)

Prefab Cooking

Many entrées could be quickly prepared if it were not for an ingredient that requires considerable cooking time. For example, if you have cooked soybeans on hand, you can swiftly complete many recipes you might otherwise have to rule out.

Many other ingredients, and recipe elements, can be prepared ahead and in quantity, so that when a recipe specifies them, no precious time is lost. The list includes piecrusts, crepes, brown rice, curry sauce, spaghetti sauce, hard-cooked eggs, cooked potatoes, grated cheeses, ground nuts, bread crumbs, and all the legumes. Many of these foods can be kept in the refrigerator for a week or longer. Some can be stored in the freezer for several months.

Do a thorough job of building this kind of a stockpile, and some meals may be more a matter of assembling ingredients than of cooking. And often, this is a most welcome situation.

Sprouts differ from all other prepared-ahead items, for they're the result of growth rather than cooking. The growing of sprouts amounts to having a small, contained farm in your kitchen. It's a farm, moreover, whose "rainfall" and temperature you can completely control, and that can therefore be depended upon to produce in abundance. In order to have a constant supply of a variety of sprouts—wheat, fenugreek, mung bean, chia, lentil, rye, alfalfa, cress, mustard—plant as frequently as you harvest. If your consumption falls short of your production, put surplus sprouts in a container with a tightly fitting cover and store in the refrigerator.

There are sound culinary and nutritional reasons for making sure that you never run out of sprouts. Both as a garnish and as a vital element in an entrée and in baked goods, the contributions of sprouts are unique. Use them generously: 2 tablespoons to ½ cup will fit nicely into a sandwich; 1 to 2 tablespoons in soups just before serving; and add 2 tablespoons to scrambled eggs just as you are about to remove them from the burner.

27

This solicitude as to just when sprouts should be added to hot foods is based on reason rather than emotion. The concern is for the vitamins that sprouts contain, vitamins damaged by excessive heat. Sprouts also, in being linked with the wonders of seeds, are themselves a nutritional marvel. A seed contains the embryo of a plant. For this embryo to develop into a plant, it must be nourished like a fetus in the womb. The seed supplies this essential nourishment—carbohydrates, proteins, and oils—and by harvesting time, they are in the sprouts, and shortly thereafter, in the consumer. They contain enzymes, too, those catalysts of vital chemical reactions in the body. As individuals age, a source of enzymes is especially important, for with age the body is less able to manufacture its own. A good supply of enzymes is actually important at all ages; and since the heat of cooking, if it is high, destroys enzymes, fresh sprouts are virtually life savers. To top off all this bounty, sprouts are low in calories. It's as though we must not have any reason—and calories would be a reason for many people—for not eating sprouts.

Your role as a sprout farmer is not arduous. All you need do is see to it that the seeds, beans, and grains that are being sprouted are kept moist and warm. There are many ways of doing this, all of them relatively simple:

1. A colander may be used to sprout seeds that are large enough not to slip through the colander's holes. Soak seeds that are to be sprouted overnight. Rinse them two to four times daily. Place colander over a large bowl, and cover it with a towel and dinner plate to retain heat.

2. Seeds may be sprouted by scattering them in a thin layer on several thicknesses of moistened paper towels placed in a shallow, nonmetallic pan. The paper towels, of course, must be kept moistened.

3. The most common sprouting method is to soak seeds overnight in a Mason jar. The lid should be fitted either with fine wire screen or cheesecloth, which is held in place by a rubber band or the jar ring. The soaking water should then be poured out, fresh water poured in, and the seeds rinsed. Be sure to invert the jar so that all water is removed. Seeds to be sprouted should be kept moist, but not left in a puddle of water.

4. One of the easiest ways—if not the easiest—is to sprout seeds on the three tiers of a Plexiglas sprouter. This sprouter, on sale in health food stores, has drainage openings on each tier and requires very little attention.

Slow cooked onions. Hundreds of recipes start off with a sliced, chopped, or minced onion sautéed in butter. Onions have the best flavor when they are cooked so slowly that they do not brown, but turn a beautiful golden color and are sweet, mellow, and tender. You may not always have the time or inclination to give them this special treatment, but if you can get into the habit of sautéing extra onions each time you need them, you'll find they are a marvelous ready-to-go ingredient. They can be kept in the refrigerator for several days in a tightly covered jar, or frozen in small amounts for a longer time, ready to add to whatever dish you have in progress.

If you have a food processor, or other mechanical slicing and chopping equipment, you can quickly and easily process a pound or so of onions, and let them quietly simmer away while you are occupied elsewhere, with only an occasional stir or progress check required. The heat should be adjusted so low that the onions do not even start to color until they have cooked about 15 minutes. The entire cooking process will take from 20 to 30 minutes. The onions will cook down to a much smaller amount than you started with, of course. One pound of onions will make about 1½ cups when done.

Sautéed onions can be used in an amazing variety of ways—with vegetables, in soups, as a topping for casseroles or patties, in sandwiches and omelets. Try them gently warmed and used as a topping for cream cheese spread on whole grain bread. Delicious!

Sautéed mushrooms. These lovely, expensive morsels are very perishable and it is sometimes difficult to use them quickly enough. If a recipe calls for less than the amount you have on hand, it's a good idea to do them all while you are about it and keep the extra in a covered jar in the refrigerator for use a few days later, or stash them away in the freezer.

The best way to wash mushrooms is to drop them into a large pan of cold water and shake them around with your hands to loosen any particles of dirt. Do this quickly so the mushrooms do not absorb water. They should then be well drained and dried in a clean kitchen towel or on paper towels. After cleaning, and trimming the ends, mushrooms can be sautéed whole, sliced, or chopped. They must be dry at the time of cooking or they will not brown well.

When you cook mushrooms, they should not be crowded in the pan and the butter should be very hot. If you are doing a large amount, or your pan is small, divide the mushrooms into several batches. To sauté a half pound of mushrooms, heat 2 tablespoons of butter over high heat in a large, heavy skillet. When the foam begins to subside (don't let it brown or burn), add the mushrooms. Toss them with a spoon until well coated with butter and continue tossing, or shaking the pan, for about 7 or 8 minutes. As soon as mushrooms are lightly browned, remove from the heat.

Duxelles. These are finely minced mushrooms that have been drained of their liquid and sautéed in butter until they are dry and brown. The result is actually the essence of mushroom flavor and can be used in countless ways. They will keep tightly covered in the refrigerator for several weeks, or they may be frozen. One half pound of mushrooms will make about 1 cup of duxelles. They can be used in omelets, sauces, stuffings, with vegetables, in soups, or just spread on crackers or toast and used as an appetizer. Freeze them in small amounts—a little goes a long way. A recipe for making duxelles can be found in the Index.

Artichokes. Stuffed artichokes are a beautiful, elegant dish, but they do take time to prepare. They are one of the longer-cooking vegetables and it is necessary to precook them and remove the inedible choke before stuffing. Therefore, having them already partially cooked, de-choked, and frozen (or refrigerated, if you will be using them within a day or two), can turn them into a quick and easy gourmet treat.

Large artichokes, about 4- to 4½-inches high and approximately the same diameter, are best for stuffing. To prepare them ahead, wash them well by shaking them around in a large pot of water. Break off the stem and the small leaves at the base. Cut off the base so that the artichoke will stand firmly upright. Turn it on its side, and with a sharp knife, cut off about a half inch of the top center leaves. With scissors, cut off the tip of each of the remaining leaves. Rub the cut parts with lemon juice and drop the artichoke into a large pot of cold water containing a tablespoon of vinegar per quart of water. This will keep the artichokes from becoming discolored while you are preparing the others.

In the largest pot you can find, boil 7 or 8 quarts of water containing 1 or 2 tablespoons of salt and 2 tablespoons cooking oil. Drop in the prepared artichokes. Bring back to boiling and cook slowly for 20 minutes. Drain and cool.

Remove the center cone of leaves and dig out the fuzzy choke (this is most easily done with a melon baller). Sprinkle the scraped area with lemon juice. Package airtight and freeze, or keep in the refrigerator for several days. A recipe for stuffing and final cooking of parboiled artichokes appears on page 146.

Dried legumes. Soybeans, chick-peas,* navy beans, lentils, split peas, etc., are a valuable source of protein in any diet. They can, however, take a long time to cook and can be discouraging to someone in a hurry.

There are several factors that affect the cooking time of dried legumes—the type of bean, age, hardness of water, and altitude. If beans have been stored too long, or at too high a temperature, they become hard and take longer to cook. Therefore, buy them only in small amounts and store in a cool, dry place, tightly covered. Beans cook quicker in soft water. If you are in a hard water area, the United States Department of Agriculture advises adding ⅛ teaspoon of baking soda to every cup of dried beans at the start of the soaking. In effect, it softens the water. Do not add any more soda than this; it will affect the nutritive value of the beans.

There are several other ways to speed up the cooking time of beans, and other legumes as well.

Quick-soak and freezing method. This is best for the longer-cooking legumes, such as soybeans, lima beans, navy beans, and chick-peas. Wash and pick over the beans. Bring water to a boil (allow about 6 cups of water for 2 cups of beans). Add the beans and when the water again comes to a boil, cook for exactly 2 minutes. Remove from the heat, partially cover the pan, and allow to stand for one hour. Drain, rinse with cold water, and drain again. Freeze.

When ready to use, thaw the frozen beans quickly under running water until they have separated.

In a large saucepan, bring a quantity of water (10 cups if you started with 2 cups of beans) to a boil. Add the beans, ½ teaspoon salt, and a small amount of butter to control the foam and enhance the flavor. Do not cover the pan. Bring the beans to a boil, lower the heat and allow the beans to cook gently until tender. The amount of cooking time required will vary according to the type of bean and other factors, but you will find that it is within 30 to 50 minutes for most. Soybeans may take a little longer. After the beans are drained, they are ready to use in your chosen recipe or may be

---

* Chick-pea in Spanish is "garbanzo." We use this name in a number of our recipes. Just keep in mind that they're the same legume.

packaged and stored in the freezer, ready for instant use when needed. It is best to undercook beans intended for freezing.

If you are wondering why we are telling you to throw away the cooking water (after all these years of being told to save it), according to Dr. Louis B. Rockland, Research Chemist with the United States Department of Agriculture, "There is increasing evidence from work in our own laboratory, as well as studies being conducted elsewhere, which strongly suggests that it would be better to discard the bean cooking water, especially for some types of beans." It is believed that the cooking water is at least partially responsible for causing the gastrointestinal distress that many people experience after eating beans. Loss of nutrients in cooking water is negligible.

To pressure-cook quick-soaked and frozen beans, follow the same preparation procedure as for regular cooking. Do not fill the cooker over half full. Process in enough water to cover the beans, with salt and butter added, at 15 pounds pressure for 3 minutes. Remove from heat and allow the pressure to drop of its own accord. If the beans are not quite tender, simmer them a little longer, partially covered, adding boiling water if necessary.

It is not absolutely necessary to freeze beans after they have been quick-soaked. You can, if you wish, get right on with the cooking after soaking, but you will probably find that they take somewhat longer to cook. The freezing has a tenderizing effect.

Lentils and split peas do not require presoaking. They can be cooked for half the usual time, then drained, rinsed, and frozen. They will cook quickly after the freezing, so it is best not to use the pressure cooker. You may end up with a purée. Of course, if you are planning a soup, that wouldn't be all bad.

One cup of dried beans will yield 2½ to 2¾ cups when cooked. Dried lentils and split peas will approximately double their volume.

Quick-cooking beans. Frozen quick-cooking beans, developed by the USDA, represent a major breakthrough in timesaving and fuel conservation. They do not have to be washed or soaked, and require only 15 minutes or less to cook to uniform tenderness. They have a smooth creamy texture, a good, fresh flavor, and are free of the paperlike skin usually found in regular beans.

A large variety of frozen quick-cooking beans is available, including limas, small white, pink, pinto, dark and light red kidney, black-eyed peas, and garbanzos. Follow the cooking directions on the package. If your recipe calls for a sauce to be used with the beans, cook the beans separately and blend the ingredients after the beans are cooked. Seasonings such as tomato sauce, vinegar, and sugar, have a tendency to harden the beans and may lengthen the cooking time. Reduce the amount of salt used since quick-cooking beans already contain some.

Also available are dried quick-cooking beans that have been treated by the same process as the frozen ones and then redried. The dry beans require about 30 minutes to cook, but they have a special appeal for campers or those with limited freezer space.

Ground dried legumes. Grinding dried lentils, split peas, or whole peas in a blender until they are a fine powder makes it easy to produce a delicious soup in just a short time. Grinding dried legumes is one task that the blender does better than the food processor.

Wash legumes and spread in a single layer in a shallow pan to dry in a 150° oven for about 10 minutes.

Grind no more than ½ cup of peas or lentils at a time and do not allow the blender to become overheated. Stop from time to time to let it cool. Try to achieve a flourlike consistency. The finer your blend, the better the results will be.

It is best to store legume powders in the refrigerator or freezer. They will keep for a while on the kitchen shelf, but once the outer coating of these legumes is broken, they tend to deteriorate more rapidly. See the Index for recipes using ground dried legumes.

Rice. Cooked rice can be a great timesaver, especially if you use the more nutritious brown rice that takes nearly an hour to prepare. Whenever you are cooking rice be sure to double the amount so you will have some left over for use in a different recipe. You can keep cooked rice in the refrigerator for several days. Cold rice salad is delicious. Cooked brown rice makes a quick and flavorful thickener for soups when whirled in the blender. To reheat rice, put it in the top of a double boiler, or in a collapsible steamer basket set over boiling water, cover and heat about 5 minutes, until it is heated through. Stir it with a fork once or twice while it is heating.

Frozen rice is another matter. It can be frozen most successfully, but in order to preserve a fresh flavor and texture, it should be cooked only half the usual length of time. Rinse it in cold water, drain and freeze. (Empty, clean plastic cottage cheese or yogurt cartons make good containers.) To reheat and serve, drop the frozen rice into boiling salted water, and when it returns to a boil, cook over lowered heat 1 minute for white rice, 3 minutes for brown. Drain it well and serve, or keep it warm in a slow oven.

Pizza. If there is enough space in your freezer, you may want to keep a supply of partially baked pizza crusts. It is much more practical to store these items already shaped and ready for the oven, because if you freeze only a lump of dough you will have to thaw it first and then shape it—all of which can take a very long time.

To partially bake a pizza, spread the prepared dough with your favorite pizza sauce, and bake it on the lowest oven shelf at 450° for about 5 to 7 minutes, until set but not browned. Remove from the oven, slide the pizza carefully out of the pan onto a rack and allow to cool. When cooled, return to the pan and place in the freezer, lightly covered with plastic wrap until frozen solid. The pizza may then be removed from the pan, wrapped for freezing and returned to the freezer while the pan goes back to the kitchen for other use.

When ready to serve, place original pan on the lower shelf of oven and turn to 450°. While the oven is heating, unwrap pizza, add your favorite topping ingredients to the crust—cheese, sautéed onions, green pepper slices, etc., and dribble with a little olive oil. Slide the frozen crust onto the hot pan and bake about 15 minutes, or until crust is lightly browned and crisp around the edges and the topping is hot and bubbling.

Piecrusts. These may be frozen unbaked or baked. They are rather fragile and should be stored in a spot where they are not likely to be crushed. They are convenient to have on hand for a quick quiche or pie.

Nuts are used extensively in vegetarian cuisine and can be very expensive if bought in small quantities. Save money by finding a store that sells them in bulk. They keep perfectly when stored in plastic bags in the freezer. Grind some in the blender or food processor so they will be ready to use in recipes that call for them. Store in small amounts in tightly closed glass jars in the refrigerator.

Cheese. Whenever possible, use only freshly grated cheese. However, for emergencies have bags or jars of grated cheese in the refrigerator or freezer to pour out and use. It's a good way to use all the little ends and bits of leftover cheese that might otherwise be wasted. All cheeses freeze except cream cheese. You can also keep uncreamed cottage cheese in the freezer for 3 or 4 months. Uncreamed cottage cheese can be blended until smooth in the food processor to make an excellent low-calorie, low-cost substitute for cream cheese.

Bread freezes beautifully. If sliced before freezing, only the amount needed can be removed without thawing the whole loaf. If you are freezing an unsliced loaf, cool it on a rack after baking and place it unwrapped in the freezer. When frozen, put in a plastic bag and seal airtight. Breads made with the refrigerated CoolRise method (developed by the test kitchens at Robin Hood Flour Company) make it possible to fill your house with the beautiful aroma of freshly baked bread just before dinner time, even though you may have mixed the dough as much as 24 hours earlier. After removing the loaves from the refrigerator, they need only a 10-minute wait at room temperature before baking. Nearly any bread recipe can be made this way by doubling the amount of yeast called for and following the CoolRise procedure. See the Index for CoolRise recipes.

Bread crumbs made from your own homemade bread are more flavorful than the packaged kind that you buy at the store. They will keep for a long time in jars in the refrigerator or can be stored in the freezer. Get into the habit of tossing all the end pieces and bits of bread that have become too dry for other use, into the blender or food processor for crumbs.

Small bread rounds are useful to have on hand for canapé bases. Occasionally, when baking bread, save some of the dough and bake it in little tomato paste cans. The tiny loaves bake quickly and can be sliced into thin rounds, toasted, spread on a tray to freeze, then packaged in plastic bags. This avoids the waste of cutting bread slices into rounds with a biscuit cutter and having scraps left over.

Vegetable stock keeps in the refrigerator for a short time, but it is much better to freeze it. It can be frozen in ice cube trays and popped into plastic bags for storage. You can remove what you need and return the rest to the freezer. The size of ice cube trays varies. To know how much stock will be in each cube, melt a cube of ice and measure the amount of water.

Tomato sauce base. When icicles are dangling from the eaves, and snow is piling up along the fence, it is delightful to bring back the glorious days of summer with the taste of fresh, vine-ripened tomatoes. Tomatoes cannot be frozen successfully for use in salads or for slicing, but they can be peeled, chopped, and frozen for use in sauces, casseroles, or soups. No canned tomato product equals their taste. If you have a supply of ripe, unblemished tomatoes, drop them a few at a time into boiling water. After a minute or two, plunge them into cold water, slip off their skins and chop by hand or in the food processor. Mix in a little lemon juice (juice of 1 lemon for 10 pounds of tomatoes) and freeze. Or, using your favorite recipe, make a cooked tomato sauce and freeze it. The sauce, of course, will be more of a time-saver later. Omit garlic and spices because freezing tends to alter their flavor, but you can include some fresh chopped herbs. The garlic and spices can be added when heating the frozen sauce for use in a recipe.

Pesto, made with fresh basil leaves, is one of the most delicious of all the Italian pasta sauces. It can also be used as a flavoring in salad dressings, with vegetables, in butters, in soups, etc. If you have access to this fragrant herb (it's very easy to grow indoors in a pot or in the garden), by all means make a pesto base and freeze it.

To make 1 cup of base, wash about 3 cups of basil leaves and dry on paper towels. Place the leaves in a blender or food processor. Add ¾ cup of high-quality olive oil, ¼ cup of pine nuts or walnuts, and 1 teaspoon salt. Blend until well homogenized. Pour into an ice cube tray and freeze. When cubes are hard, remove them to a plastic bag and store in freezer.

If basil leaves are unavailable, parsley may be substituted. The Italian flat-leaved variety has the best flavor.

For details on how to turn this pesto base into a sauce for pasta, see Index.

Precooked vegetables. Most vegetables are at their peak when freshly cooked. Keeping them warm for any extended period will overcook them, and that means losing precious nutrients, as well as fresh color, texture, and flavor. Many times, however, especially when entertaining, it's inconvenient to cook vegetables at the very last minute.

The answer? Cook them in advance—and still have them at their peak. Here's how:

Steam the vegetables in a collapsible steamer basket until barely crisp-tender. Do not overcook. Then immediately plunge them into a large pot of iced or very cold water. Use a lot of water so it doesn't warm up. The point is to stop the cooking almost instantly, lock in nutrients, color, and flavor, and keep the texture firm. Drain and refrigerate immediately. When ready to serve, melt butter in a heavy pan, add seasonings and vegetables and toss until heated through.

Vegetables prepared in this way will taste and look as if just cooked. The reason is, they are not overcooked. They're at their freshest, most flavorful best! The water used for steaming may be saved for your vegetable stockpot.

Phyllo, sometimes called fillo, filo, or filla, and also known as "strudel leaves" (the Greeks do not believe in standardization), is a dough made of flour, water, and salt and rolled into fragile, tissue-thin leaves. It is a useful, ready-made pastry that can be quickly fashioned into ethereally beautiful dishes, as delightful to look at as they are to eat.

Using phyllo will present no problems once you have handled it and understand its requirements.

1. It must be brought to room temperature before handling. Therefore, you must remember to take it out of the freezer the night before you plan to use it, or out of the refrigerator several hours beforehand. Since it keeps for weeks in the refrigerator if tightly sealed in its plastic bag, we recommend keeping it there. However, once opened, the package should be kept in the freezer. If you have forgotten (as we sometimes do) to take the leaves out of the refrigerator ahead of time, you can remove them from their plastic bag, wrap and *seal tightly* in foil, and place in a *very low* oven (below 150°) for 15 to 20 minutes. They can be warming while you prepare the melted butter and filling.

2. Phyllo must not be allowed to dry out while you are working with it. Unfold the stack of leaves carefully and cover it with a sheet of plastic wrap. Remove the leaves one at a time as needed, keeping the rest covered with plastic. Place the first leaf on a slightly dampened cloth. Brush it with melted butter. You need not cover every inch with butter—just a few broad swipes with a wide pastry brush. Remove the second leaf, place it on top of the first, brush with butter. Continue this procedure, using as many leaves as your recipe directs.

3. Phyllo pastry must be handled with a light, delicate touch. Otherwise it will break, shred, or rip and you'll be tearing your

hair. If you are rolling the layers of leaves around a filling that will puff up during baking (one that contains eggs, for example), do not roll too tightly or the filling will burst through the pastry.

When baked, the layered, thin pastry leaves form an incredibly fragile, crisp, delicately golden crust. They are used extensively in Greek and Turkish delicacies, but after you have tried them you will want to experiment with creating your own masterpieces. Phyllo can be bought in Greek and gourmet food shops.

Salad greens and leafy green vegetables. Make a habit of trimming and washing greens, eliminating excess water, and storing in plastic bags in the refrigerator as soon as possible after purchase. Not only will they stay fresh and green much longer, but having them all ready to toss into a salad or saucepan is a great time-saver. Some greens and vegetables (like watercress, parsley, and asparagus) keep longer if they are placed upright in a glass or jar with their stems resting in water and a plastic bag over the top.

Whipped cream is a favorite embellishment for many desserts. To eliminate the nuisance of having to whip it up at the last minute, beat a sizeable amount of cream, sweetened or flavored as you wish, and spoon dollops of it on waxed paper spread over a cookie sheet. Freeze these dollops until solid, then peel away the waxed paper and put them into plastic bags until needed. They can be arranged on the dessert before dinner and will have softened to eating consistency by the time you are ready for them.

Roux. When roux, a mixture of flour and butter that has been cooked together, is added to liquid (usually milk), it becomes a "white sauce." White sauce is often used as a thickener in soufflés, soups, casseroles, and sauces, such as béchamel, hollandaise, etc. Stopping in the middle of a recipe to make a roux can be a nuisance. It also takes precious time. Here is a way to get around it. When you find it necessary to make roux, go wild—cook up a large amount and freeze the excess. It will take no more time than making a few spoonfuls, and the same amount of fuel.

To make the roux, melt 1 cup of butter (½ pound) in a heavy-bottomed saucepan over low heat. Blend in 1 cup of flour and cook slowly, stirring for 2 or 3 minutes until the mixture is pale gold, frothy, and lightly bubbling. You now have a roux. Allow to cool a few minutes and then drop it by tablespoons onto a foil-lined cookie sheet. The roux will spread out into thin wafers. Freeze, uncovered, until solid. Peel off the foil, drop the wafers into a plastic bag and return them to the freezer.

To make a thin white sauce, use 1 wafer of frozen roux per cup of hot liquid. For a medium sauce, use 1½ wafers. For a thick sauce, use 2 wafers. As a soufflé base, use 3 wafers. Drop the appropriate number of roux wafers into your hot liquid; stir vigorously with a wire whisk over a moderately high heat until thickened.

Appetizers and Snacks

Most people enjoy eating with their hands. It probably harks back to the ancient communal pot, and it offers a basic pleasure, like watching an open fire, dining outdoors, sitting on the floor, or going barefoot. Part of the appeal of appetizers and snacks may very definitely be that many of them are finger foods.

Appetizers, as a prelude to a meal, are meant to sharpen the appetite, not destroy it. For that reason, they should be quite simple and not too numerous. But they may also be served as a first course, or even the main event, and then they can be more substantial. There are occasions when it is fun to make a whole meal from a variety of savory tidbits. Serve a selection of fillings and a basket of warm pita bread, arranged for guests to help themselves and invent their own original combinations, and you can create a delightfully entertaining event as well as provide a nourishing meal.

Snacks for the after-game or after-theater crowd, the backpacking hiker, the children home from school, or the person who just doesn't feel like having a full meal, can also be nutritious as well as hunger satisfying.

FRUIT AND CHEESE

The simplest appetizers are often the most welcome. This one is as simple as it sounds—crisp, cold fruit slices presented with thin slices of sharp or mild cheese. If you want to introduce an additional taste sensation, add a bowl of Chura or Flavored Nuts (pages 64–65).

PREPARATION TIME 5 MINUTES   4 SERVINGS

    4   **large, cold apples (firm, tart eating variety), or 4 firm, ripe Bartlett pears**
    ½   **pound cheese, thinly sliced**
        Lemon juice

Wash and core apples or pears. Cut into ½-inch slices. Dip slices in lemon juice and arrange on a platter, alternating and overlapping with slices of cheese. Serve.

Note: To be really relaxed about this, simply offer a bowl of apples or pears, or a combination of the two, and let each person add the cheese to the fruit slices as he cuts them. Bunches of white grapes and a pot of brandy-flavored or wine-flavored cheese with a spreading knife are good additions to the scene.

RAW VEGETABLE PLATTER

An assortment of raw vegetables, along with a dip or spread, has become a popular party appetizer with a special appeal for dieters. Carefully arranged, the raw vegetable platter can be a delight to the eye. Use only the freshest of vegetables—young and crisp—clean them well, and for greatest enjoyment, serve them on a bed of crushed ice. Here are some that are especially good, with a few suggestions for preparing them.

Belgian Endive: Slice in half lengthwise and separate into individual leaves. These are a natural for scooping up dips, or they can be stuffed with your favorite dip or spread.

Carrots: Peel and cut into sticks, or leave whole and cut gashes part of the way through along the length. Break off sections to eat.

Cauliflower: Break off flowerets and either serve whole or slice them thinly crosswise. To crisp, soak in ice water about 10 minutes. Drain and keep covered in refrigerator until used.

Celery: Cut into strips or chunks. Soak in ice water, drain and chill.

Cherry tomatoes: If stem ends are fresh and green, leave them on. Otherwise, remove. For a different taste, try dipping them in oil and rolling in chopped fresh basil or dill.

Cucumbers: Use young ones with not too many seeds. Peel if waxed (most that you buy in the store are) and cut into strips.

Fennel: Remove leafy portions and reserve for use in salads. Separate stalks and cut into slices.

Green peppers: Cut in half and remove all seeds and the white membrane. Cut in sections, vertically.

Kohlrabi: Peel and cut into sticks.

Mushrooms: Leave small white mushrooms whole. If using larger mushrooms, cut sections through the cap vertically, just to the stem. Break apart sections to eat.

Radishes: Cut off the root ends but leave on a bit of the stem and a few tiny leaves if they are fresh and green.

Romaine: The very center leaves of romaine or iceberg lettuce make wonderful scoops for dips.

Scallions: Cut off ends and remove outer skin. Trim neatly.

Turnips: Peel and cut into sticks.

Zucchini: Use very young, fresh squash. Cut off ends and cut cross-wise into small sections. Or cut part of the way through, preserving the shape intact, and break into sections for eating.

STUFFED EGGS À LA GRECQUE

The fresh taste of lemon and mint gives these stuffed eggs a deliciously different twist. Dwarf lemon trees are one of the easiest of house plants to grow, and will reward you all year round with fragrant blossoms and a small harvest of fruit. You'll be able to use their grated zest (the yellow part of the peel), knowing that it is free of chemical fumigants that are used on nearly all store-bought lemons to prolong their life in storage.

PREPARATION TIME 5 MINUTES   **MAKES 16 HALVES**
COOKING TIME 10 MINUTES

    8   eggs

Cover eggs with cold water in a large saucepan, bring to a boil, and cook slowly for 10 minutes. Cool quickly under running cold water, peel and cut in half lengthwise. Remove yolks, set aside whites.

    3   tablespoons mayonnaise
    1   tablespoon yogurt
    1¼ tablespoons lemon juice
    ½   teaspoon grated lemon peel (optional)
    1   teaspoon chopped fresh mint

Place yolks in a small bowl and mash well with a fork. Add mayonnaise, yogurt, lemon juice, peel (if used), and chopped mint. Blend all together with a fork and fill reserved whites. Served chilled.

Note: If fresh mint is unavailable, use ½ teaspoon dried mint leaves and crush them into the lemon juice. Let stand a few minutes, then strain out the leaves and add juice to other ingredients.

GARLIC STUFFED EGGS

When garlic is slowly cooked, it loses its sharp bite and becomes smooth and mellow. Nine cloves of garlic may sound like a lot, but it's no mistake.

PREPARATION TIME 5 MINUTES   MAKES 12 HALVES
COOKING TIME 10 MINUTES

- 9   cloves garlic, peeled
- 6   hard cooked eggs

In a small saucepan, cover the garlic with water and bring to a boil. Reduce heat and cook slowly 10 minutes. Drain, transfer to a small bowl and mash the cloves with the back of a spoon, or use a mortar and pestle. Slice eggs in half lengthwise, remove yolks and add to the bowl, stirring and blending into the garlic. Set aside whites.

- ¼   teaspoon lemon juice
- 1   tablespoon finely chopped dill pickle
     Salt and pepper to taste
- 3   tablespoons olive oil or salad oil
     Paprika
- 1   tablespoon chopped parsley

Add lemon juice, dill pickle, salt, and pepper to the bowl and blend all ingredients together with a fork. Slowly dribble in the oil, beating with a fork until the mixture is smooth and pasty.

Fill the egg whites with this stuffing, dust with paprika, and sprinkle with chopped parsley. Serve chilled.

BOUREKAKIA

These unbelievably fragile, crisp, cheese-filled appetizers are a traditional Greek delicacy. They are best served while still warm, but can be made ahead and frozen, then reheated. They take a *little* longer to make than some of our other appetizers, but are so special we couldn't resist including them. See page 37 for information on the care and handling of phyllo dough.

PREPARATION TIME 20 MINUTES   MAKES ABOUT 24 APPETIZERS
BAKING TIME 15 MINUTES

1	3-ounce package cream cheese
¼	pound feta cheese, crumbled
1	cup cottage cheese or ricotta cheese
2	egg yolks
	Few gratings of nutmeg
1	tablespoon chopped parsley

Combine all ingredients in a food processor or blender, or beat together in a bowl until smooth.

¼	cup (½ stick) butter
9	sheets phyllo dough

Melt the butter in a small pan. Remove 3 sheets of phyllo from package, keeping the rest of the dough covered with plastic. Lay one sheet of dough on a slightly dampened cloth with the long side toward you. Brush it lightly with butter in long, sweeping strokes. (The entire sheet does not have to be covered with butter.) Lay second sheet on top of first and brush with butter. Repeat with third sheet.

Spread a ribbon of ⅓ of the cheese mixture along the edge near you, leaving a margin of 1½ inches along the edge and two sides. Fold the bottom edge up over the cheese and turn in the two sides. Using the dampened cloth as an aid, roll the phyllo up loosely as for a jelly roll. Repeat with the rest of the phyllo and filling.

Place seam side down on an ungreased cookie sheet, spaced well apart. Bake at 375° about 15 minutes until golden brown and flaky. Allow to cool 10 minutes, then cut into 2-inch pieces. Serve while slightly warm or at room temperature.

If made ahead and frozen, allow to thaw. Heat in 375° oven 15 minutes, until crisp.

Note: This recipe works well with other fillings too. Here's another favorite. It can be made in a flash when there are some presautéed onions and mushrooms and a few hard-cooked eggs in the refrigerator. If the filling is divided between two rolls instead of three, it can make a delicious and elegant main course:

PÂTÉ EN FILO

PREPARATION TIME 15 MINUTES   MAKES ABOUT 24
BAKING TIME 15 MINUTES

- ¼ cup slow-cooked chopped onions (page 29)
- 1 tablespoon oil
- ½ pound mushrooms, sliced and sautéed
- ½ pound walnuts, ground
- 2 hard-cooked eggs, chopped
- ¼ teaspoon tarragon
  Salt and pepper
  Sour cream (as needed)

Brown the onions lightly in oil. Add mushrooms and heat, stirring a moment or two. Place in food processor or blender and add remaining ingredients except sour cream. Process, turning on and off and scraping down the sides until well mixed but not completely smooth. Moisten with sour cream.

Follow the same procedure as in making Bourekakia. If it is to be used as a main course, cut in large portions.

HOT MUSHROOMS

Quickly sautéed mushrooms are an elegant appetizer. Use only those that are very fresh and white, wipe them clean with a damp paper towel and trim stem ends. Mushrooms must not be wet when you add them to the butter. They take only a few minutes and should be served immediately.

PREPARATION TIME 5 MINUTES   4 GENEROUS SERVINGS
COOKING TIME 5 MINUTES

- 4 tablespoons butter
- ½ pound fresh white mushrooms, cleaned and trimmed
- 1 clove garlic, minced
- ¼ teaspoon freshly grated nutmeg
  Salt to taste
- 1 tablespoon lemon juice

In a wide, heavy skillet, heat butter over moderately high heat until foam starts to subside. Do not allow butter to brown. Add mushrooms, tossing to coat in the liquid. Stir in all remaining ingredients *except* the lemon juice. Stirring often, sauté for 5 minutes, or until mushrooms are cooked but still firm. Sprinkle over and blend in the lemon juice. Serve with picks for spearing.

FROG IN THE POND

This is a snack to delight the whole family—especially the younger members. Perhaps the name provides the fascination, but it tastes very good, too. Warm the sauce while the eggs are cooking.

PREPARATION TIME 4 MINUTES   4 SERVINGS
COOKING TIME 7 MINUTES

    4   slices whole grain bread
    2   tablespoons butter

With a 2-inch biscuit cutter, or a small juice can with top removed, cut a hole in the center of each bread slice. (Save the centers to use as canapé bases. You can store these in the freezer and use when needed.) Melt butter on heated griddle, and toast slices until lightly browned on one side.

    4   eggs
        Tomato sauce, heated

Turn bread slices over and break an egg into each hole. Cook until eggs are set on the bottom. Turn bread to other side and cook until egg is of desired firmness. Arrange on plates and spoon warm, spicy tomato sauce over.

RIPE OLIVE-CHILE-CHEESE SNACKS

These savory, crunchy morsels can disappear so quickly, you might think they evaporated. Cut into wedges, they can serve as appetizers. Or, with a bowl of hot soup, they can provide lunch. Canned green chiles vary in size and hotness. Use your judgment after tasting, to decide how much of them to include.

PREPARATION TIME 5 MINUTES   4 SERVINGS OF
BROILING TIME 5 MINUTES   2 HALVES EACH

 4   English muffins
     Butter

Split, toast, and butter the muffins.

 2 to 3 canned green chiles, rinsed, seeded, and chopped
 ¼   cup mayonnaise
 ⅔   cup grated cheddar cheese
 ⅓   cup sliced, pitted ripe olives
 ¼   teaspoon prepared mustard
     Chopped parsley

Stir together chiles, mayonnaise, cheese, olives, and mustard. Pile equal amounts of the mixture on each muffin half. Place on a cookie sheet and slide under broiler until cheese melts and mixture is puffed and bubbling. Sprinkle with chopped parsley and serve.

DAY LILIES

If you're the fun-loving type—as you surely must be—we'd like to suggest that you try our special "wild day lily appetizer." This is seasonal, of course—June and July—and day lilies aren't available everywhere, but if you are in the right spot, make the most of it.

As you probably know, wild day lilies are beautiful, orange flowers that grow in drifts along country roadsides, in fields, and in some people's yards. There are cultivated hybrid day lilies, too, but they don't seem to have as much flavor. Tiger lilies which have black spots, are not the same as day lilies. Day lilies bloom for one day only—hence their name—but produce blossoms in great abundance over a period of several weeks. We used to wander around, surreptitiously pinching off a few here and there (along the road—not in people's yards), but finally grew so fond of them that we planted our own, donated by a friend who had too many.

There are other edible wild flowers, but these are the only ones to which we've become really attached. Don't go around sampling flowers indiscriminately. Some of them are lethal. If you'd like to investigate this subject further, there are books, such as Euell Gibbons' *Stalking the Wild Asparagus*, that tell which plants are safe to eat.

In gathering your day lilies, cut them off as far down as you can without damaging the other blossoms. If you've gathered them from a dusty spot, you'll want to rinse them lightly. Ants think they are good, too; so you'd better check.

Arrange the blossoms in a large, shallow bowl filled with ice cubes or crushed ice. The stems are very short so the flowers will nestle directly on the ice, and if there are enough, will completely cover it. They will look dramatically exotic, and it is fun to watch the expressions of the uninitiated as they cautiously bite into the crisply tender stems and work their way up to the petal tips. The flavor is delicate, but sweet and subtly spicy. The texture is a sheer delight. Sorry to get so carried away, but we really like them.

Day lilies may seem to be more fantasy than food, but Orientals, who are very wise, have long considered them a valuable food source, as well as a delicacy.

You'll probably want to offer a little something in addition—wine, cheese, and fruit, perhaps, but you couldn't produce an appetizer much quicker or easier. Low in calories, but high in entertainment value. And anything that tastes so delicious must have some beneficial trace elements lurking in there somewhere!

CALZONE

Calzone (rhymes with baloney) is a relative of the ubiquitous pizza. It is, in fact, a puffy turnover made with pizza dough. Since calzone is meant to be eaten in the hand, it is excellent for snacks, picnics, or informal entertaining. This version has a light, fluffy filling made with ricotta and egg, but the possibilities for other stuffings are endless.

PREPARATION TIME 20 MINUTES   6 SERVINGS
BAKING TIME 20 MINUTES

1   recipe Lazy Day Pizza (page 186)

After the 10-minute rising period, punch down the dough, knead once or twice, and divide dough into 6 pieces. Form each piece into a ball, and roll or pat each ball into a 6- or 7-inch circle.

1   egg, slightly beaten
1   cup ricotta cheese
¼   cup grated Parmesan cheese
¼   cup chopped parsley
      Pinch of nutmeg

In a large bowl, thoroughly mix the egg, ricotta, Parmesan, parsley, and nutmeg. Place several tablespoons of this mixture in the center of each round of dough, dividing the amount of filling equally.

½ to ⅔ cup shredded mozzarella cheese

Sprinkle mozzarella over the filling, fold the dough circles in half to enclose, and press down the edges to seal securely.

Olive oil

Place calzone on a lightly greased baking sheet, brush the top of each turnover lightly with oil, and bake at 425° for 15 to 20 minutes, or until puffy and toasted around the edges.

Variations: Another good filling is one that contains ingredients usually found in pizza topping. On each dough round, spread some tomato sauce and top it with sautéed chopped green peppers, onions, mushrooms, or anything else you like. Add some shredded mozzarella and a sprinkling of grated Parmesan cheese. Fold, seal, and bake as above. Calzone is also delicious made with the dough and filling for Mostly Mushrooms Pizza.

QUESADILLAS

In Mexico, one of the most popular snacks is the quesadilla. It is a little turnover, made with a tortilla, and can have a variety of fillings. Our favorite is stuffed with green chiles and Jack cheese. If the tortillas are dry, they must be softened by heat before they are folded over the filling. To do this, pat the tortillas with dampened hands, and place on a moderately hot griddle, turning them constantly until they are soft and warm, about ½ minute. If left on the heat too long, they will become brittle, and impossible to use for quesadillas.

PREPARATION TIME 5 MINUTES   6 SERVINGS
BAKING TIME 10 MINUTES

>   2   canned green chiles
>   ½   pound Jack cheese, cut into thick strips
>   6   corn tortillas*
>   Butter or oil (optional)

Rinse the chiles under cold running water, washing out the seeds. Drain on paper towels and cut into thin strips. Place a strip of cheese and as many strips of chile as you wish in the center of each tortilla, fold over and place on a medium-hot, lightly greased griddle. You may have to hold the folded edge of the tortilla in position with tongs until it has baked a minute or two. When lightly browned on one side, turn quesadilla to other side until browned and the cheese melted.

Variation: If you prefer a crisper result, fry the folded, stuffed tortilla in a skillet in a small amount of hot butter or oil.

* Available frozen in supermarkets.

Crackers

What could be better—or simpler—than a mellow, ripe wedge of fine cheese and a basket of crunchy, homemade crackers still warm and fresh from the oven? Making crackers is so much fun, and so quick and easy to do, that you may never again want to go back to the store-bought variety, once you've tasted what you can turn out. And they don't contain a trace of chemical additives!

CRACKED WHEAT WAFERS

PREPARATION TIME 12 MINUTES   MAKES ABOUT 24 WAFERS
BAKING TIME 10 TO 15 MINUTES

- 1   cup unbleached white flour
- 1   teaspoon baking powder
- ½   teaspoon salt
- ¼   cup cracked wheat
- ¼   teaspoon poppy seeds

Sift flour, baking powder, and salt into a large bowl. Stir in cracked wheat and poppy seeds.

- 2   tablespoons cold butter
- ½   cup ice water or less

Cut butter into flour mixture until well blended. Quickly but lightly, stir in as much water as you need to make a dough that holds together. Divide dough into two parts and form each into a ball.

Pat each ball into a rectangle on a lightly floured board, and with a rolling pin, roll out to tissue thinness. Cut with a 2-inch biscuit cutter. Bake wafers on an ungreased cookie sheet at 350° about 10 minutes, or until crisp. Do not allow them to scorch. Cool on a rack and store in an airtight container.

JANE'S WHEAT WAFERS

PREPARATION TIME 12 MINUTES   MAKES ABOUT 30 WAFERS
BAKING TIME 10 TO 15 MINUTES

- 1½ cups whole wheat flour
- ½ cup soy flour
- ½ teaspoon salt
- 1 teaspoon baking powder
- 1 tablespoon poppy seeds

Mix dry ingredients well with a fork.

- ¼ cup oil
- ½ cup ice water or less

Blend in oil and add enough water to make dough. Divide dough into four parts and roll each paper thin. Cut with a 2-inch biscuit cutter. Bake on ungreased cookie sheet at 350° until golden and crisp. Cool on a rack and store in an airtight container.

SESAME SNAPS

PREPARATION TIME 12 MINUTES   MAKES ABOUT 20 CRACKERS
BAKING TIME 10 MINUTES

- 1½ cups rye flour
- ¼ cup soy flour
- ¼ cup raw or toasted sesame seeds
- ¾ teaspoon salt
- 1 teaspoon baking powder

Stir together flours, seeds, salt, and baking powder, mixing well.

- ¼ cup oil
- ½ cup ice water or less

Dribble in oil and blend well. Add water, tossing with a fork until of doughlike consistency.

Form into a ball and divide into four parts. Roll each tissue thin on a lightly floured board. Cut with a 2-inch biscuit cutter. Bake on an ungreased cookie sheet at 350° until crisp. Cool on a rack and store in an airtight container.

CHAPATTI CHIPS

PREPARATION TIME 4 MINUTES   MAKES ABOUT 24 CHIPS
BAKING TIME 4 MINUTES

- ½   cup unprocessed bran
- 1   cup whole wheat flour
- ¼   cup toasted sunflower seeds, finely chopped
- 2   tablespoons butter

Combine dry ingredients in a large bowl and add the butter. Mix well with the fingers until crumbly (or use a food processor).

½ to ⅔ cup water

Slowly dribble in enough water and knead to form a smooth ball of dough. On a lightly floured surface, roll out *very* thin and cut with a 2-inch biscuit cutter or small jar cover. (Or, divide dough into 24 parts and roll each into a marble. Flatten between palms to desired thickness.) Bake on a hot, ungreased griddle until crisp, turning several times during baking. Cool and store airtight.

Note: ½ teaspoon salt may be added to the dough, but when Chapatti Chips are eaten with cheese, lack of salt is not noticeable.

Spreads and Dips

The most important thing to remember about spreads and dips is that they should have a good consistency—not so thin that they drip, or so thick that they are hard to scoop or spread.

Leftovers make wonderful appetizer spreads. A cup or two of cooked vegetables, plus a few additions, can be whirled in a food processor or blender to a smooth, colorful pâté—and no one will guess that it was left from last night's dinner.

Here are a few combinations that may suggest still others to you.

DUXELLES

Duxelles (Doo-zell) is a versatile, exciting substance created by the French. It can be used in so many ways that it is difficult to know just where it belongs in this book. However, since it makes a beautifully simple, yet sophisticated, appetizer when spread on thin toast or crackers, we decided to put it here. See page 30 for further discussion of duxelles.

PREPARATION TIME 7 MINUTES   MAKES ABOUT 1 CUP
COOKING TIME 8 TO 10 MINUTES

   ½   **pound fresh mushrooms, washed and dried**

Finely mince the mushrooms by hand or in a food processor. Gather the mushrooms, a few tablespoons at a time, into the corner of a double thickness of cheesecloth, or other clean cloth, and twist very hard to extract the juice into a small bowl. (Save this liquid for use in soups, sauces, or cooking vegetables.)

   3   **tablespoons unsalted butter**
   2   **tablespoons minced shallots or scallions**

Melt the butter in a large, heavy-bottomed skillet over moderately high heat. Add mushrooms and shallots and cook, stirring often, until the mushrooms are lightly browned and the liquid disappears.

       Salt and pepper

Add salt and pepper to taste. Allow to cool. Place in a tightly covered glass jar and refrigerate or freeze.

NUT BUTTERS

With the help of a food processor, you can make your own nut butters. In addition to the familiar peanut butter, you can produce smooth, exotic-tasting spreads from almonds, cashews, hazelnuts, walnuts, macadamia nuts . . . Butters may be made from raw or roasted nuts, salted or unsalted.

Process up to 2 cups of nuts, stopping occasionally to scrape down the container as the nuts climb up its sides. As the processing continues, the nuts will form a paste that gathers itself into a ball, whirls briefly around the container and then disperses. At this point, stop the motor and scrape down the container. If the consistency is not smooth enough, continue processing until desired texture is reached. The longer the nut paste is processed, the smoother it will become, as oils are released. If the butter remains too dry (some nuts are oilier than others), blend in a tablespoon or two of oil or butter. Salt may be added if you wish. Two cups of nuts will make about 1 cup of butter. The butter should be refrigerated.

RAW MUSHROOM SPREAD

The subtle, wild taste of raw mushrooms is tantalizing when captured as a spread on toasted whole wheat bread or crisp whole grain crackers.

PREPARATION TIME 5 MINUTES   **MAKES ABOUT 1 CUP**

- 1   8-ounce package cream cheese
- 1   tablespoon chopped chives

In mixer, food processor, or by hand beat cheese and chives together until smooth and creamy.

1¼ cups finely chopped fresh mushrooms
     Salt
- 2   tablespoons minced parsley

Stir in mushrooms and add salt to taste. Mound in small serving bowl and sprinkle with parsley or other fresh herb.

SCHWARTZE TEIVEL

This appetizer is an all-time family favorite. Its name, which means "black devil," was given it by Grandmother, who used to char the eggplant on the gas stove flame. Of course, the eggplant would split and the juice that dribbled out would burn and be the very "devil" to clean up. We have altered her method by using the broiler instead of the stove top, and by placing the eggplant in an old aluminum ice-cube tray with the dividers removed. Disposable aluminum foil pans work well, too.

In selecting your eggplant, heft several until you find one that feels light in relation to its size and has a shiny, smooth black or purple skin.

Schwartze Teivel has Middle Eastern origins. There are many versions.

PREPARATION TIME 5 MINUTES　　　　　　　　　**MAKES ABOUT 1½ CUPS**
BROILING TIME 20 MINUTES

   1   medium-sized eggplant

Wash eggplant, but don't cut off ends or peel. Poke a few holes in it with a large fork (so it won't explode in the oven and live up to its name), and place in a pan under the broiler. Broil for 10 minutes, turn and broil 10 more minutes, or until the skin is well charred and the pulp is *very* soft. When cool enough to handle, peel back the skin and with a large spoon scoop the pulp out into a small bowl. With the same spoon, chop and stir until the consistency is fairly smooth and uniform.

   ½   teaspoon salt
   ¼   teaspoon freshly ground black pepper
   1 to 2 tablespoons olive oil or to taste
   ⅓   cup finely chopped onion
   1   tablespoon sesame seed

Add above ingredients and blend with a spoon or fork.

Note: Schwartze Teivel may be served at room temperature or chilled. It is delicious on wheat crackers or toasted rye rounds as an appetizer, or makes a delightful salad topping on crisp, cold lettuce leaves and slices of avocado and tomato. We often toss in some sliced radishes for a lively color and crunch. Sliced ripe olives are a good addition, too.

WHITE BEAN DIP

PREPARATION TIME 4 MINUTES   MAKES ABOUT 1 CUP

1¼ cups cooked dried white beans or chick-peas
3   tablespoons lemon juice
½   cup olive oil

Put beans, lemon juice, and oil in container of blender or food processor. Whirl until smooth and blended, stopping motor occasionally to push the mixture down into the blades. Add a little water if mixture is too thick.

1   small clove garlic, minced
    Salt and pepper

Add garlic, salt, and pepper and blend again. Serve garnished with toasted sesame seeds or pine nuts.

24 KARAT PÂTÉ

PREPARATION TIME 4 MINUTES   MAKES ABOUT 1½ CUPS
COOKING TIME 5 MINUTES

2   tablespoons butter or margarine
¼   cup sliced or chopped onion
1   clove garlic, minced
½   teaspoon curry powder

Melt the butter or margarine in a heavy pan over moderately low heat. Add the onion and garlic and cook slowly until soft and limp, stirring occasionally. Stir in curry powder and cook a few more seconds. Place in blender or food processor bowl.

1¾ cups cooked carrots
6   tablespoons cashew butter (page 58)

Add carrots and cashew butter to onion mixture and process until smooth. Taste for seasoning. Add salt if needed.

¼   cup coarsely chopped cashews

Stir in chopped cashews. Serve at room temperature with crackers or crisp, raw vegetables. If made ahead, cover and chill. Bring to room temperature before serving.

MUSHROOM BUTTER

A bit of nutmeg gives this pale, creamy spread a delicate, intriguing flavor that is very special. For an extra treat, spread it on toasted French bread rounds, and slide them under the broiler for a moment or two until bubbly.

PREPARATION TIME 7 MINUTES   MAKES ABOUT 1¾ CUPS
COOKING TIME 7 MINUTES

4   tablespoons unsalted butter
½   cup finely chopped onions
½   pound fresh mushrooms, thickly sliced

Melt butter in large, heavy frying pan. Add onions and cook over moderately low heat for 2 minutes. Add mushrooms, tossing and stirring to coat with butter. Sauté 5 minutes.

⅛   teaspoon freshly grated nutmeg
½   teaspoon salt
1   tablespoon lemon juice
⅛   teaspoon freshly ground black pepper
4   teaspoons butter

Stir in nutmeg, salt, lemon juice, pepper, and butter. Cook, stirring, until butter melts and seasonings are blended. Place mixture in blender or food processor and blend.

4   tablespoons grated Parmesan cheese

Add cheese to blender and process again. Scrape mixture into a jar, cover and chill.

Snack Mixtures

Mixtures of dried fruits, nuts, seeds, and cereals are lightweight, quick-energy sources for the hiker, biker, student, and office worker. With wine or other beverages, they can also serve as appetizers. Exact amounts and proportions are unimportant in some of these blends. They can all be made in a few minutes.

BACKPACK SNACK

Wheat or rye flakes*
Raw sunflower seeds
Raw sesame seeds

Toast the flakes, sunflower seeds, and sesame seeds in an ungreased skillet. Pour into a bowl.

Whole or chopped nuts
Raisins
Dried fruits, chopped

Add nuts, raisins, and dried fruits to the bowl. Cool the mixture completely. Carry in tightly closed plastic bags or other containers.

TROPICAL FRUIT AND NUT MIX

Dried pears, chopped
Dates, pitted and chopped
Dried banana chips
Cashew nuts, broken
Coconut, dried, unsweetened
Raisins

Blend all ingredients and package airtight.

* Available at health food stores.

SPROUT SNACKS

These attractive morsels are great to keep on hand in the refrigerator for an after-school recharger or whenever the munchies strike. They are nourishing as well as delicious.

PREPARATION TIME 5 MINUTES   **MAKES 12 SNACKS**

- **4** tablespoons cream cheese
- **1** cup chopped sunflower seeds or nuts
- **⅔** cup sprouted wheat*
- **½** cup raisins

Beat the cream cheese with a fork until soft and creamy. Stir in seeds, sprouts, and raisins and blend well. Shape into 12 small balls.

Wheat germ

Roll in wheat germ and serve, or cover and chill.

And here's another good combination:

- **½** cup cream cheese
- **⅓** cup alfalfa, cress, or mustard sprouts*
  Pinch of curry powder
- **½** cup chopped salted peanuts

Blend the cheese, sprouts, and curry powder. Form into balls and roll in chopped nuts.

*See Index for sprouting information.

FLAVORED NUTS AND SEEDS

Highly nutritious nuts and seeds make tasty little nibbles just as they are. For extra flavor and enjoyment, however, toast them in the oven with a blend of spices and other seasonings. Use raw nuts and seeds that have not been previously roasted and salted. English walnuts, pecans, cashews, almonds, peanuts, filberts, and dried, hulled sunflower, pumpkin, and squash seeds all make excellent appetizers when prepared this way.

PREPARATION TIME 2 MINUTES   MAKES 1 CUP
ROASTING TIME 12 TO 13 MINUTES

1   cup shelled nuts* or dried seeds

Spread nuts or seeds in a shallow pan in a single layer. Toast in a 350° oven until golden, about 10 minutes. Stir often.

1 to 2 teaspoons salad oil
One of the following seasoning mixtures:

MEXICAN: **1 teaspoon chili powder, ½ teaspoon ground cumin, ¼ teaspoon ground coriander, ¼ teaspoon salt, dash of cayenne pepper.**

INDIAN: **½ teaspoon ground turmeric, ¼ teaspoon ground coriander, ¼ teaspoon cayenne pepper, ¼ teaspoon salt, ⅛ teaspoon garlic powder.**

CHINESE: **½ teaspoon Chinese 5-spice powder, ¼ teaspoon salt, or to taste.**

HERB: **¼ teaspoon each crumbled rosemary, thyme, and oregano; ½ teaspoon salt, ¼ teaspoon cayenne pepper.**

Sprinkle the nuts or seeds with salad oil and stir in one of the seasonings suggested (or your own original blend). Return to oven for 3 minutes, stirring to combine flavors well. Let stand to cool and crisp. Store in an airtight container.

*English walnuts should be blanched before toasting to remove their astringency. Drop them in boiling water and boil for 3 minutes. Drain and dry on paper towels before proceeding.

CHURA

This is an adaptation of a spicy Indian snack. We doubt if they ever use sunflower seeds in theirs, and certainly not Rice Krispies, nor would they make it so mild as ours. If you like it hotter, just increase the amount of turmeric and cumin, or add a dash of cayenne pepper or chili powder.

PREPARATION TIME 3 MINUTES   MAKES 2 CUPS
COOKING TIME 3 MINUTES

    2   tablespoons salad oil
    1   teaspoon ground coriander
    ½   teaspoon ground cumin
    ½   teaspoon ground turmeric
    ¼   teaspoon dry mustard

In a large, heavy frying pan, heat the oil over a moderate flame. Stir in the combined spices and blend into the oil until well heated. Remove pan from heat.

    1   cup Rice Krispies
    ½   cup salted Spanish peanuts
    ½   cup roasted, salted cashews
    ⅓   cup raisins
    ¼   cup roasted sunflower seeds
    ¼   teaspoon ground cloves

Mix all ingredients and stir into spiced oil to blend the flavors. Allow to cool. This will keep about 1 week if stored in an airtight container.

Pocket Bread Sandwiches

There are endless combinations of savory morsels that can be used to stuff the flat, chewy bread with a pocket known as pita. One pleasant way to entertain casually, at lunch or brunch, is to provide a variety of ingredients or mixtures, along with shredded lettuce and chopped tomatoes, and allow each guest to create traditional or unconventional stuffings for the pocket bread. It's fun for everyone and very little work for the host.

Below, we offer several mixtures that we have enjoyed. Consult the Index for a pita bread recipe.

AVOCADO POCKET SANDWICH

PREPARATION TIME 12 MINUTES   **4 SERVINGS**

1	ripe avocado
½	cup chopped cucumber
½	cup chopped cauliflower
½	cup sliced mushrooms
½	cup diced or shredded Monterey Jack cheese
¼	cup Italian dressing

Dice ½ the avocado. Reserve the other half. Toss diced avocado, cucumber, cauliflower, mushrooms, and cheese with Italian dressing.

2	large or 4 small pita breads
1	teaspoon lemon juice
½	cup chopped tomato

Cut the pitas in half if large, or slit halfway around the edge and separate if smaller size, and pull the edges apart to form a pocket. Fill each with ¼ of the mixture. Mash the remaining avocado with a fork and stir in the lemon juice and tomato. Spoon mixture inside each sandwich.

SPICY TACO PITA

PREPARATION TIME 5 MINUTES   6 SERVINGS
COOKING TIME 15 MINUTES

- **4**   tablespoons slivered almonds

Place almonds in heavy-bottomed frying pan and toast over moderate heat until golden, shaking pan occasionally. Remove nuts from pan and set aside.

- **2**   tablespoons cooking oil
- **¼**   cup chopped onion

In the same pan, heat oil and stir in the chopped onion. Cook until limp and translucent. Pour off excess fat.

- **3**   cups cooked kidney beans, mashed
- **½**   cup tomato sauce
- **½**   cup water
- **2**   canned green chiles, rinsed, seeded, and chopped
- **¼**   cup raisins
- **½**   teaspoon oregano
- **¼**   teaspoon ground cumin
    Salt and pepper to taste

Into the sautéed onion, mix kidney beans, tomato sauce, water, chiles, raisins, oregano, cumin, salt, and pepper. Cook, stirring, until liquid had evaporated. Fold in the almonds.

- **1**   cup diced or shredded Jack cheese
- **2**   cups shredded lettuce
    Tomato slices, halved
- **3**   large pita breads, halved

Arrange cheese, lettuce, and tomato slices in separate bowls. Spoon the hot bean mixture into the pockets of the pita bread and top with cheese, lettuce, and tomato.

POCKETFUL OF GOLD

PREPARATION TIME 10 MINUTES   4 SERVINGS

6   large hard-cooked eggs

Peel and chop eggs coarsely with a fork, pastry blender, or in a food processor.

⅓   cup mayonnaise
½   teaspoon salt
1½   teaspoons Dijon mustard
¼   teaspoon freshly ground black pepper
3   tablespoons chopped nuts
2   tablespoons sliced or chopped pitted ripe olives
2   tablespoons chopped sweet green pepper

Gently blend all ingredients together.

2   large pita breads, halved
     Alfalfa sprouts

Pile the egg mixture into pockets of the bread halves. Garnish with alfalfa sprouts.

Soups

Aeons ago someone said, "A soup—to be good—has to be cooked slowly and for a long, long time." This was then repeated—endlessly. Someone also put that same thought concerning soup in writing, and it was copied diligently by scribes. Thus myths are created.

Despite this, our emphasis on soups will be on speed and ease of preparation. We will also have our sights set on soups that are nutritious and therefore healthful. Not only is this possible in a meatless soup, but richness of flavor and aroma can be achieved with herbs and spices and vegetable stock.

Such a stock is paradoxical; for it is both priceless and without cost. How this can be is simple: the delicious, life-sustaining stock is made of vegetable trimmings. Fifty minutes of simmering extracts all their flavor, and a sieve separates stock from pulp. Frozen in an ice-cube tray, the stock can be used, as many cubes at a time as are needed. For more immediate use, simply keep the stock in the refrigerator. (If, by some mischance, you have no stock on hand, you may use water or an instant vegetable broth powder from the supermarket or health food store, following package directions to prepare. But don't expect the results to be as satisfactory as good, homemade stock.)

Start making your stock now. We also want to advise you, when you make soup, to prepare a big pot of it. If you don't, the soup will all be consumed on the first day, and there'll be none for the second day when it is, cliché notwithstanding, even better.

CURRIED PEA SOUP

A beautiful, pastel green soup, it's fragrant and delicious—appealing to the sight and to the senses of smell and taste. Even hearing comes into play when the lip smacking and the requests for seconds start. When you serve seconds, or midway through the first, for a new taste sensation add a dollop of sour cream and a sprinkling of minced chives.

PREPARATION TIME 7 MINUTES   SERVES 4
COOKING TIME 5 MINUTES

- 1   cup fresh or frozen peas
- 1   medium onion, quartered
- 1   medium carrot, cut lengthwise
- 1   clove garlic
- 1   stalk celery with leaves
- 1   medium potato, quartered
- ½   teaspoon salt
- 1   teaspoon curry powder
- 4   tablespoons butter
- 1   cup stock

Cook all ingredients in pressure cooker for 2 minutes and then put them in the blender. Blend at high speed for 10 seconds.

- 1   cup milk
- 1   cup water
       Minced parsley
       Sour cream (optional)
       Chopped chives (optional)

While the blender is still running, pour milk and water into container. Turn blender off after 20 seconds and pour its contents into the pressure cooker. Heat on medium heat, without the cover. Serve with garnish of minced parsley.

PEA-D-Q SOUP

Here we present sanity's answer to the commercial instant soup. This soup of ours that is made in 12 minutes has, we shall argue, been made instantaneously. More importantly, the instant reaction to our soup has been most favorable.

PREPARATION TIME 5 MINUTES   SERVES 2 TO 3
COOKING TIME 7 MINUTES

> 2   cups stock

Bring stock to a boil.

> 1   medium onion, chopped
> 1   large clove garlic, minced
> 2   tablespoons butter

Sauté onion and garlic in butter for 5 minutes. Set aside.

> 4   tablespoons powdered split peas (page 33)

Mix powder in enough cold water to form a paste. Stir it into the boiling stock. Reduce heat to keep stock at a simmer. Stir occasionally to prevent peas from sticking to bottom of pan.

> ¼   teaspoon salt
>   Pepper to taste
> ⅛   teaspoon chervil
>   Sprinkling of dillweed
> ¾   cup peas, fresh or frozen

Add sautéed mixture, seasonings, and peas to soup. Simmer a minute or so—or until ready to serve, if that's longer.

> **Grated cheddar cheese**

Garnish each serving generously with the cheese.

SPANISH BORSCHT

In Spain, when the weather is inclement (hot), the natives take to gazpachos. There is a plural form of this word, because there are many gazpacho soups. No matter what form the soup takes, it's cold, made up only of raw vegetables, and favors a variety of condiments. Obviously, it's a soup that you can modify in any way your taste suggests. Here's an especially easy-to-make gazpacho on which you might like to improvise.

PREPARATION TIME 7 MINUTES   **SERVES 6 TO 8**

1	green pepper, seeded and chopped
1	small onion, chopped
1	cup chopped cucumber
1	large clove garlic, crushed
1	quart tomato juice
¼	cup salad oil or olive oil
¼	cup vinegar
2	tablespoons lemon juice
1	tablespoon brown sugar (not packed)
1	tablespoon honey

Mix these ingredients by hand, or at slow speed in an electric mixer.

½	cup milk

As all the ingredients are being mixed, slowly pour in the milk. It may curdle if added too quickly.

½	teaspoon dry mustard
	Pepper to taste
1	cup plain yogurt (or more)

Stir in seasonings and yogurt. Chill for 15 minutes in the freezer or up to 24 hours in the refrigerator. Or you may serve the soup with an ice cube in the center of each serving. Try these garnishes: cubes of avocado, hard-cooked egg slices, chopped scallion tops, croutons.

SPLIT PEA SOUP SANS SOUCI

Tracy, Bill's eighteen-year-old daughter, loves soup. Of the various split pea soups he has prepared, she prefers the simplest and easiest. And we agree with her choice. No celery. No onions. Simply split peas, potatoes, butter, salt, a sprinkling of dillweed, and oregano.

PREPARATION TIME 5 MINUTES   MAKES ABOUT 3 QUARTS
COOKING TIME APPROXIMATELY 30 MINUTES

> **1   pound split peas**

Wash peas by putting them in a large mixing bowl and swirling them quickly with one hand, around and around, as cold water runs into the bowl from the faucet. Pour water off and repeat swirling process until peas appear a bright, clean green. (All legumes can be cleaned effectively by this method.)

> **15 cups stock**
> **1½ teaspoons salt**

Put stock and salt in soup pot, add split peas and bring to a boil.

> **3   medium potatoes**

Peel potatoes, cut into chunks and add to pot.

> **4   tablespoons butter**
> **Dillweed**
> **Oregano**

Add butter, dillweed, and oregano to soup 5 or 10 minutes before soup is done—when potatoes are soft and split peas have virtually become liquid.

FRESH TOMATO SOUP

When your garden becomes a cornucopia of tomatoes, make this soup. We even found it to be good using supermarket winter tomatoes that were well ripened. Obviously, this is a delicacy for all seasons. However, when tomatoes are expensive, Tomato and Rice Soup or Spanish Borscht can serve as substitutes.

PREPARATION TIME 5 MINUTES   SERVES 3
COOKING TIME 15 MINUTES

    1   medium onion, chopped
    2   tablespoons butter

Sauté onion in a heavy saucepan until soft.

    6   tomatoes, sliced
    2   tablespoons tomato paste
    1   teaspoon chopped fresh dill
    ¾   cup stock

Add these ingredients to the sautéed onion and simmer, covered, for 10 minutes.

    2   teaspoons sugar
        Salt and pepper to taste
        Minced dill or basil (optional)

After adding seasonings, whirl the soup briefly in blender or food processor. Reheat and serve with a sprinkling of fresh herb.

TOMATO AND RICE SOUP

A remarkably simple soup with an astonishingly complex flavor. It's difficult to believe that its base is nothing more than prosaic tomato juice.

PREPARATION TIME 5 MINUTES   SERVES 2 GENEROUSLY
COOKING TIME 7 MINUTES

    2   **tablespoons chopped onion**
    2   **tablespoons butter**

Sauté onions in butter for 5 minutes in a saucepan.

    3   **cups tomato juice**
    1   **cup cooked brown rice**
    ¼   **cup cream**
         Sprinkling of basil
         Sugar to taste

Add tomato juice, rice, cream, and seasonings to sautéed onion and heat to simmering point. Remove from heat and serve.

Variations: For fewer calories and a more piquant soup, yogurt—in generous amount—may be substituted for the cream. And corn may be used instead of rice.

TOMATO-SOY SOUP

This is a high-protein delicacy for the hungry. If, for some deep subconscious reason, you're prejudiced against soybeans, we assure you they are totally disguised in this soup by all the other ingredients. Easily made, and a meal in itself.

PREPARATION TIME 5 TO 7 MINUTES   SERVES 3 TO 4
COOKING TIME 10 MINUTES

    1   **small onion, chopped**
    1   **stalk celery, chopped**
    2   **tablespoons oil or butter**

In frying pan, sauté onion and celery in oil or butter for 5 minutes.

2 cups canned tomatoes
1 cup cooked or canned soybeans
  Parsley to taste
1 teaspoon salt
  Few turns of pepper grinder

Place the sautéed vegetables and the above ingredients, in the order given, in the blender. Blend at low speed at first; then at high for 30 seconds. Pour into saucepan and heat to the simmering point.

Sour cream (optional)
Yogurt (optional)

When served, some might like this soup topped with one of these garnishes.

POTATO-CORN SOUP

Though this soup may suggest corn chowder, as Scrambled Eggs Potato Soup reminded nonvegetarians of clam chowder, it stands on its own as a soup. The cheese in it is far more than a garnish. It provides both flavor—subtle though it is—and nourishment.

PREPARATION TIME 5 MINUTES   SERVES 4
COOKING TIME 3 MINUTES

1 potato, peeled and diced
1 medium onion, chopped
2 tablespoons butter
1 cup canned whole kernel corn
1 cup stock
3 cups milk
1 teaspoon salt
  Few turns of pepper grinder

Place all ingredients in pressure cooker, without rack, and pressure-cook for three minutes.

Grated Parmesan cheese
Minced chives

At time of serving, top with a generous amount of cheese, and chives.

SCRAMBLED EGGS POTATO SOUP

Vegetarians are dogged by individuals who ask, "The way you eat, where do you get your protein?" Well, here's a recipe that proves you can even have a nonmeat soup rich in protein. We've been told it tastes very much like clam chowder.

PREPARATION TIME 5 MINUTES   SERVES 6 TO 8
COOKING TIME 2 MINUTES

- 2 medium potatoes, peeled and finely diced
- 3 cups stock
- 3 cups milk

Put potatoes and liquids in pressure cooker with rack removed, and pressure cook for 2 minutes. Remove cover and reduce heat to warm. If pressure cooker is not used, cook potatoes in saucepan until tender.

- 2 slices whole wheat bread

Cut bread in small squares and add to pressure cooker or saucepan.

- 3 eggs

Add eggs to soup one at a time, whipping briskly with a fork after each addition, until egg is dissolved in liquid.

- 1 tablespoon butter
  Salt and pepper to taste
  Minced parsley

Add these ingredients, stir and serve.

VIRTUALLY UNBEATABLE BEET SOUP

This soup may not have the authenticity of the steppes of Russia, but it evokes crusty black bread and other sturdy, nutritious, peasant fare. Forget calories this once and top with sour cream; if you just can't forget, use yogurt. For a more nutritious soup, try variation below.

PREPARATION TIME 7 MINUTES   SERVES 4 TO 6
COOKING TIME 3 MINUTES

- **2** cups fresh or canned beets
- **2** carrots
- **1** medium onion
- **1** cup shredded cabbage
- **3** cups stock
- **1** teaspoon salt
  Few turns of pepper grinder
- **3** tablespoons butter
- **1** tablespoon lemon juice
  Sour cream (optional)
  Yogurt (optional)

Cut up vegetables coarsely and put them and other ingredients in pressure cooker without rack. Cook 3 minutes. Put half of the carrots and beets in blender with a cup of the stock in which they were cooked. Blend for 30 seconds. Return to pressure cooker and keep on low heat. Serve with topping of sour cream or yogurt.

Variation: After contents of blender have been returned to pressure cooker, beat up an egg, add a spoonful of the soup liquid to the egg and beat. Add a half dozen more spoonfuls, beating after each addition. Then put egg mixture in the pressure cooker and stir. Makes a richer, milder soup. If any is left over, it may be eaten cold.

HOT WEATHER BORSCHT

Borscht comes in two temperatures, hot and cold, with or without a boiled potato. This cold beet soup is a beautiful shade of pink. Instead of garnishing it with a potato, which would take extra time, we brazenly recommend adding to its creamy richness by topping each serving with a generous dollop of sour cream.

PREPARATION TIME 7 MINUTES   SERVES 6

    1½ cups sour cream
        Very thick slice lemon, peeled
        Thick slice medium onion, peeled
    ½   teaspoon salt
    1   cup cooked or canned beets, sliced

Put all ingredients in blender or food processor. Blend.

    1   cup crushed ice
        Sour cream

Add ice and blend. Serve very cold, garnished with sour cream.

VEGETABLE STEW SOUP

The sort of hearty soup that has special appeal on a cold, blustery day. Assuming you have cooked lima beans on hand, it can be made very quickly. The hard-cooked egg garnish makes the soup even more substantial, even more welcome.

PREPARATION TIME 5 MINUTES   SERVES 3
COOKING TIME 5 MINUTES

    2   carrots
    1   large onion
    1   stalk celery
    1   cup stock or water

Cut vegetables in large pieces and put in pressure cooker. Add liquid and pressure-cook 3 minutes.

1   **small green pepper, diced**
1   **cup cooked lima beans**
1   **teaspoon salt**

Put these in blender with cooked vegetables and blend until smooth. Transfer to pressure cooker.

2   **tablespoons butter**
¾   **cup milk**
      Pinch dillweed, chervil, oregano

Mix with ingredients in the pressure cooker. Heat to simmer, uncovered.

2   **hard-cooked eggs, sliced**

Garnish with eggs.

MILK OF MUSHROOM SOUP

If you like the unique flavor of mushrooms, you'll surely enjoy this soup. The other ingredients enhance the mushroom quality rather than blanket it. To be savored like an aperitif.

PREPARATION TIME 7 MINUTES   **SERVES 2**
COOKING TIME 10 MINUTES

3   **tablespoons butter**
6   **medium mushrooms**
½   **small onion**

Melt butter in small skillet. Cut mushrooms and onion into large pieces and sauté for 5 minutes.

3   **cups milk**
3   **tablespoons whole wheat flour**
1   **teaspoon salt**
      Pepper
      Grated nutmeg

Put these ingredients, in the order given, into blender. Add sautéed mushrooms and onions. Blend until smooth—about 30 seconds. Pour in a saucepan and heat. When soup has reached simmering stage, reduce heat to warm. It can stay on this heat while rest of meal is being prepared.

LEMON LIMA BEAN SOUP

Lemon and olive oil are standard Greek soup ingredients. When their distinctive flavors are combined with the others in this rich soup, they're enough to transport one to a sensualist's heaven. Nutritionally, what lima beans lack as a complete protein—a solitary amino acid—can be taken care of by the contributions of the rest of the meal (for example, Ensalada con Huevos).

PREPARATION TIME 5 MINUTES　　　　　　　　　　　**SERVES 4 TO 5**
COOKING TIME 7 MINUTES

　2　large onions, chopped
　2　cloves garlic, minced
　½　cup olive oil

Sauté onions and garlic in oil in a large, heavy saucepan.

　2　cups cooked dried lima beans
　2　tablespoons tomato paste
　¼　teaspoon thyme
　1　teaspoon salt
　1　quart stock

Add lima beans and other ingredients to the sautéed vegetables. Bring to a simmer.

　　Juice of ½ lemon
　　Minced parsley

At time of serving, stir in lemon juice and top each serving with parsley.

ZUCCHINI YOGURT SOUP

Perhaps zucchini and yogurt is less newsworthy than a chocolate cake that makes use of zucchini. Be that as it may, zucchini—in both instances—is a taste enhancer. Cold and tangy, this soup is just right on a hot day. What's more, since the yogurt isn't subjected to heat, no harm comes to its friendly, vitamin-B producing bacteria.

PREPARATION TIME 5 MINUTES   SERVES 4
COOKING TIME 10 MINUTES
TIME NEEDED TO CHILL

> 1   large onion, chopped
> 1   clove garlic, minced
> 4   tablespoons butter

Sauté onion and garlic in butter for 5 minutes.

> 2   cups stock
> 2   medium zucchini (about 1 pound), diced
> ½   teaspoon salt
>   Pepper

Bring stock to a boil in a saucepan. Add to it sautéed vegetables, zucchini, salt, and pepper. Simmer 5 minutes.

> ⅛   teaspoon curry powder
> ⅛   teaspoon thyme

Add either or both spices to soup according to taste. Cool, then chill soup in freezer up to 30 minutes. (It might be a good idea to use timer, in order not to forget that the soup is in the freezer.)

> 2   cups yogurt

When soup is ready to be served, stir in yogurt.

PIZZA SOUP
(A "pizza" you eat with a spoon)

This recipe isn't a substitute for pizza. It merely suggests pizza—gustatorily. It's a hearty soup, one that some will regard, with satisfaction, as a complete meal.

PREPARATION TIME 10 MINUTES   SERVES 6
COOKING TIME 12 MINUTES

- 4   tablespoons butter
- 1   medium onion, chopped
- 2   stalks celery, chopped
- 1   clove garlic, minced

Sauté vegetables in butter 5 minutes.

- 1   cup elbow macaroni

Cook according to package directions but don't overcook. Drain and set aside.

- 3   cups stock
- 2   cups cooked dried lima beans
- 3   tablespoons tomato paste

Combine with sautéed ingredients in a saucepan.

- 1   carrot
- 1   cup cooked dried lima beans
- 1   cup stock

Put in blender and blend. Mix with other ingredients in saucepan and bring to a simmer.

- 4 to 6 sliced mushrooms
- ½   teaspoon salt
-     Pepper to taste
- ¼ to 1 teaspoon oregano
-     Grated Parmesan cheese or slivered mozzarella

Add mushrooms, seasonings, and reserved macaroni to the soup. Serve topped with Parmesan cheese or mozzarella. If you use mozzarella, cut it in thin slivers—best done with an electric knife. Another way is to blend mozzarella and pieces of whole wheat bread in blender. The cheese is easier to handle in this form, since slivers of mozzarella tend to stick together.

THE GRAND LEFTOVER SOUP

If you've been too proud to save leftovers, or have exiled them to the rear of your refrigerator until they've spoiled, this soup should change all that. Any combination of leftovers works. And just about all you need do is blend them with milk or cream and seasonings.

PREPARATION TIME 5 MINUTES   SERVES 4
COOKING TIME 15 TO 20 MINUTES

> 1   medium onion, chopped
> 4   tablespoons butter
> ½   cup stock

Sauté onion in butter for 5 minutes in large, heavy saucepan. Add stock or water and cook for 3 minutes.

> 1   cup leftover vegetables* (Include legumes if you wish.
>   Cooked potatoes and/or cooked brown rice add body to
>   the soup.)
> 1   cup milk

Add vegetables and milk to the cooked onions, put them in blender and blend until smooth. Pour back into saucepan.

> 1½   cups stock

Add stock to vegetables in saucepan and simmer 5 to 10 minutes.

*No need to use precisely 1 cup of vegetables. If you use more, you can always correct consistency, if necessary, by adding more milk. If you don't have enough leftovers, you can supplement what you have with freshly cooked vegetables.

ONION-CHEESE SOUP

Our Jane, aged twenty, observed that this soup amounts to a cheese sandwich in liquid form. She then hastened to add, lest what she had said be taken for criticism, "I *love* it!" You'll love it, too; everyone does.

PREPARATION TIME 7 MINUTES   SERVES 3 GENEROUSLY
COOKING TIME 12 MINUTES

> 2   medium onions, finely chopped
> 2   tablespoons butter
> 2   tablespoons whole wheat flour

Sauté onions in butter in large, heavy saucepan for 5 minutes. Stir in flour thoroughly.

> 1½ cups water

Add water to the roux gradually, stirring all the while. Simmer 5 minutes.

> 1½ cups milk
> 1   teaspoon salt
>   Pepper to taste

Add milk and seasonings to saucepan and bring to a boil.

> 1   cup coarsely grated cheddar cheese

Stir cheese into hot mixture until it dissolves.

> 2   slices whole wheat toast, buttered
>   Minced parsley

Place one piece of toast on top of the other. Cut the toast into narrow strips, and then cut across them to make croutons. Put equal amount of croutons into three bowls. Ladle soup over croutons, sprinkle with parsley and serve.

SUPER-PROTEIN LENTIL SOUP

Actually soybeans should share top billing with lentils in this soup, for soybeans play an important role. Both provide protein. Together, they impart a totally new and intriguing taste. A soup for the famished gourmet—and for everyone else.

PREPARATION TIME 10 MINUTES   SERVES 6
COOKING TIME 10 MINUTES

- ½   cup washed lentils
- 4   cups stock
- ½   cup cooked brown rice
- 1   teaspoon salt

Blend lentils and 1 cup of the stock in blender until lentils are pulverized—about 1 minute at high speed. Pour into soup pot. Add remaining stock, the rice and salt. Bring to a simmer on medium heat.

- 1   medium onion, chopped
- 1   large clove garlic, minced
       Olive oil as needed

Sauté onion and garlic in olive oil for five minutes. Add to lentil and rice mixture.

- 1   cup cooked soybeans
- 2   tablespoons tomato paste
       Pepper to taste
       Grated Parmesan cheese

Add soybeans, tomato paste, and pepper to the pot and stir. Bring to a simmer and serve. For added protein thrust and taste luxury, sprinkle each portion with Parmesan cheese.

MILK (OR CREAM) OF CARROT SOUP

Smooth as a malted milk, this soup calls for the help of both pressure cooker and blender. They work wonderfully as a team. No additional utensils are needed, which reduces the amount of cleanup time. Jane—still in college—said she would grade this one A+.

PREPARATION TIME 5 MINUTES   SERVES 4
COOKING TIME 5 MINUTES

4	large carrots
1	medium onion
1	stalk of celery
1	cup water

Cut carrots lengthwise down the center and then cut these two pieces in half. Quarter the onion and slice celery in several large pieces. Put these vegetables in pressure cooker with water. Cook for 3 minutes. Place in blender.

½	cup cooked brown rice (Having the cooked rice on hand makes for easier, quicker preparation.)
1	cup milk (Cream may be used, though the milk does very nicely.)
1	teaspoon salt
	Sprinkling of ground pepper

Add these ingredients to the contents of blender. Hold hand lightly on blender top. Blend until smooth, 30 seconds. Return to pressure cooker. (If some vegetables adhere to sides of blender, wash them from sides with a little added milk.)

4	tablespoons butter

Add butter. Heat on low to medium heat in uncovered pressure cooker. This soup can also be served cold.

Salads and Salad Dressings

Use the term "main course," if you wish. We implore you, however, not actually to regard the main course as literally the main part of a meal, as being able—by itself—to satisfy completely and sustain life. For one thing, this wouldn't be fair to salads. We feel strongly that salads should not be relegated to an insignificant role in anyone's menu.

Once, iceberg lettuce was synonymous with salad—an angular chunk of it cut from a head, positioned in the center of a plate and daubed with mayonnaise. Growers and shippers pushed iceberg lettuce because of its superior staying qualities. Now, all sorts of leafy greens are available—romaine, the two B's, Bibb and Boston, escarole, chicory, watercress, et cetera. And we've gone a long way in what we regard as acceptable to enhance the greens—sprouts, cheese, seeds, nuts, fruits—on and on to the imagination's horizon. What's more, there's no longer a need to use the same old bottled dressings. New ones can be whipped up quickly in the blender as required.

The intention of this brief introduction is to indicate how important and pleasurable a part salads can play in the vegetarian cuisine. From Plata de Frutas to Improvisational Greek Salad, we trust the recipes will serve as a catalyst to arouse your culinary creativity.

GAZPACHO SALAD

This slightly spicy, molded salad is a favorite of Manners West, a twig of our family living in California. In an earlier chapter, we referred to one of our soups as "a pizza you eat with a spoon." Well, here's a soup you can eat with a fork!

Agar-agar powder, available in most health food stores, is an easy-to-use, tasteless gelatin substitute made from seaweed. There are several forms of agar-agar, any of which may be used for this recipe. We have used the powdered variety. If you use one of the other forms, you will have to adjust the procedure to fit the package directions. If you want to shorten the setting time, the filled mold may be placed in the freezer for 30 minutes.

PREPARATION AND COOKING TIME 15 MINUTES   **SERVES 6**
SETTING TIME ABOUT 2 HOURS

4	cups tomato juice
1	tablespoon agar-agar powder
1	tablespoon chopped fresh basil or 1 teaspoon dried basil
1	tablespoon lemon juice
¼	teaspoon Tabasco

Bring tomato juice to a boil, sprinkle agar-agar over the surface and simmer, stirring with a wire whisk, for 5 minutes. Remove from heat and add the basil, lemon juice, and Tabasco.

½	cup chopped celery
½	cup chopped green pepper
½	cup grated carrot

Stir all the vegetables into the tomato juice mixture. Rinse a 6-cup mold with cold water and pour in the gazpacho. Allow to cool to room temperature and place in the refrigerator until set.

2	medium cucumbers, peeled and sliced
	Sour cream
	Chopped fresh dill

To unmold salad, loosen around the edge with a knife, dip bottom of mold in hot water briefly, hold a serving dish over the top and invert. The salad should drop out easily. If it does not, repeat dipping. Surround the salad ring with sliced cucumbers and serve with sour cream and dill.

IMPROVISATIONAL GREEK SALAD

Be prepared to feel as though you're living in Greece, during the Golden Age of Pericles. Creativity, after all, is this salad's most important ingredient. Your inventiveness comes into play both in the selection of the vegetables and in their arrangement. For Grecian symmetry, you might have a line of overlapping sliced mushrooms at each end of a platter. And each time you make this salad, it should be different—in content and appearance.

Instead of preparation time, we thought it would be better to offer a suggestion as to the best procedure for assembling this salad with dispatch: 1. Clean all the vegetables to be used. 2. Slice them. 3. Arrange them. 4. Season them. Different dressings for different items provide pleasing gustatory surprises. When possible, use the dressings you have on hand.

Here's one Greek Salad we prepared as a guide—also to be made and enjoyed, and to encourage you to try your hand at making *your* Greek Salad.

SERVES 4

1   head iceberg lettuce (Romaine, salad bowl, or spinach may be substituted or used in addition)
1   medium onion, thinly sliced
8   mushrooms, cleaned and sliced
6   cherry tomatoes, halved
1   unpeeled cucumber, sliced
2   hard-cooked eggs, sliced
2   cups cooked garbanzo beans

Arrange attractively on a large platter as suits your fancy.

¼   cup vinegar, sweetened with sugar
2   tablespoons lemon juice
½   cup sour cream
¼   cup Classic French Dressing
      Salt and pepper
      Feta cheese
      Cracked wheat bread toast

Put the sweetened vinegar on the cucumber slices, the lemon juice on the garbanzos, the sour cream on the cherry tomato halves, the French dressing on the mushrooms, and the salt and pepper on the egg slices. Crumble feta cheese over everything. Serve with thick slices of toasted cracked wheat bread, buttered generously.

After such a healthful salad, we felt we might indulge in a hedonist's dessert: Rich Chocolate Pudding topped with Quick Vanilla Ice Cream.

FIT-FOR-A-KING CABBAGE SALAD

One more readily associates cabbages with kings, than with pineapples and peanuts. As a consequence, one is intrigued by the novelty of this salad and pleased by how good all of it tastes. Children—and the young in heart, generally—take special delight when they happen upon a peanut or a morsel of pineapple.

PREPARATION TIME 5 MINUTES   SERVES 6

- 4 cups shredded cabbage
- 1 8¼-ounce can crushed pineapple, drained
- ½ cup salted peanuts

Toss together cabbage, pineapple, and peanuts in a salad bowl.

- ½ cup sour cream
- 1 teaspoon sugar
- ¼ teaspoon celery seed
- ¼ teaspoon salt
   Freshly ground black pepper to taste

Combine sour cream and seasonings and pour over cabbage mixture. Toss all together and refrigerate until served.

ANTIPASTO SALAD

Fresh, colorful vegetables lightly cooked in a spicy tomato sauce flavored with herbs and then chilled are a traditional appetizer course in Italy. Served on a bed of lettuce, and accompanied with hard-cooked egg halves (or stuffed eggs), and/or an assortment of cheeses, they become a complete meal salad, or the perfect companion to a simple pasta dish.

PREPARATION TIME 10 MINUTES

COOKING TIME 8 TO 10 MINUTES

CHILLING TIME SEVERAL HOURS OR OVERNIGHT

SERVES 4 AS A MAIN COURSE

OR 6 AS A SIDE DISH

2	8-ounce cans tomato sauce
½	cup catsup or chili sauce
½	cup olive oil
⅓	cup lemon juice
1	teaspoon dried oregano
1	teaspoon dried basil
2	teaspoons prepared horseradish
1	large clove garlic, crushed

In a large, heavy saucepan, combine above ingredients and simmer slowly while you prepare the vegetables.

2	medium-sized zucchini, cut into ¼-inch slices
2	large sweet red or green peppers, seeded, membranes removed, cut lengthwise into ½-inch slices
1	9-ounce package frozen artichoke hearts, thawed and drained
3	stalks celery cut into 1-inch pieces
1	cup fresh mushroom caps

Add vegetables and mushrooms to sauce, cover and simmer, stirring occasionally until they're tender, but still crisp, 8 to 10 minutes. Remove from heat, uncover and allow to cool, then cover and chill for several hours or overnight.

Lettuce
Sliced pitted ripe olives

Serve on individual lettuce-lined plates, lifting the vegetables from the sauce with a slotted spoon, and topping each serving with a small amount of the sauce and a garnish of sliced ripe olives.

DILLED CARROTS

Salads that can be made ahead and kept in the refrigerator for several days are a real convenience. They're especially useful, when entertaining, for buffets. Bright orange carrot slices and crisp white onion rings, flecked with snipped green dill, might earn a place on the table for beauty alone. But we all know that carrots are good for us, and this salad tastes even better than it looks.

PREPARATION TIME 12 MINUTES   SERVES 6
CHILLING TIME 1 HOUR OR LONGER

>   8   large carrots
>   Boiling water

Peel carrots with a swivel peeler and cut into ¼-inch slices. Place in steamer basket over boiling water and steam until just tender— about 7 minutes. Plunge immediately into cold water. Drain well, and turn into a serving bowl.

>   1   medium mild onion, thinly sliced
>   2   tablespoons finely chopped fresh dill
>   ⅔   cup Classic French Dressing, made with 3 tablespoons lemon juice and 1 tablespoon distilled white vinegar
>   1   clove garlic, crushed (optional)
>   1   teaspoon celery seed (optional)

Separate the onion into rings and add to the carrots. Sprinkle with dill. Pour the dressing over the vegetables. If you wish, add a crushed garlic clove and 1 teaspoon celery seed to the dressing. Cover salad and chill. If chilled longer than an hour, remove from refrigerator 30 minutes before serving.

HOT SLAW

For coldslaw to be hot is something of a contradiction. But hot slaw's very good, and that's the main thing.

PREPARATION TIME 5 MINUTES   SERVES 4
COOKING TIME 7 MINUTES

- 4 tablespoons (½ stick) butter
- 4 cups shredded cabbage

Melt butter in a saucepan. Add cabbage and stir until cabbage is well coated with butter.

- 2 tablespoons water
- 1 teaspoon salt

Add water and salt to the saucepan. Cover, bring to steaming point, then reduce heat and simmer for 6 minutes.

- 2 tablespoons sugar
- 2 tablespoons vinegar
- ½ teaspoon dry mustard

Stir these into the cabbage. Cover and cook for 1 minute. Remove from heat.

- ½ cup sour cream

Blend in the sour cream and serve hot.

LENTIL SALAD

This is a delicious main course salad, rich in protein.

Lentils are smaller and more tender than they were back in the old days, and don't need to be presoaked. If you can find the tiny red ones (in a health food or gourmet shop), you may be surprised at the short cooking time they need. In fact, if you don't watch them carefully, you'll end up with a kettle of lentil mush. If it happens, just make lentil patties instead of salad. They'll be delicious. Standard lentils take around 40 minutes. Taste them after 20 minutes. They should be cooked until just tender. If you are using previously cooked lentils for this dish, reheat them a few minutes in the steamer basket before adding the dressing and other ingredients. For the best flavor, the salad should stay overnight in the refrigerator.

PREPARATION TIME 10 MINUTES   SERVES 8
COOKING TIME 20 TO 40 MINUTES

- 2   cups lentils (or 4 cups hot, cooked lentils)
- 1   clove garlic, crushed
- ¼   teaspoon salt
- 3   tablespoons wine vinegar
- ½   teaspoon dry mustard
- ⅔   cup olive oil
      Freshly ground pepper
      Pinch ground cloves
      Dried herbs (tarragon or basil)

Cook lentils, drain, and keep warm. Mix garlic with the salt and mash thoroughly together with the back of a wooden spoon. Beat in the vinegar and dry mustard. Place mixture in a small glass jar with screw top and add oil, a few grinds of pepper, cloves, and a pinch or two of herbs. Shake well to blend. Toss the lentils with the dressing.

- 2   small onions, thinly sliced
- 1   sweet green pepper, seeded and diced

Add vegetables and toss again. Taste for seasoning. Refrigerate.

Suggestion: Serve surrounded with stuffed eggs, alternating with quartered tomatoes, and sprinkled with bits of chopped pimiento and chopped scallions. On the buffet table, Gazpacho Salad and Lentil Salad make a good team.

MIDDLE EASTERN BREAD SALAD

Instead of croutons in their salads, chefs in the Middle East often use split, toasted, and broken loaves of Pocket Bread. This bread salad is a blend of garden-fresh vegetables, seasoned in the Mediterranean style.

PREPARATION TIME 15 MINUTES   SERVES 4 TO 6

- ½ cup Lebanese Salad Dressing
- 2   medium-sized tomatoes, diced
- 1   cucumber (peeled, if waxed), sliced
- 1   sweet green pepper, seeded and cut into strips
- 4   green onions (scallions) chopped, including tops
- 1   carrot, scraped and shredded
- 6   radishes, sliced
- 1   small head lettuce (iceberg, romaine, escarole, etc.) or a mixture of several kinds, torn into bits

Pour salad dressing into a large salad bowl. Add all ingredients, ending with the lettuce. Do not toss. Cover bowl with plastic wrap and refrigerate until serving time.

- 1   large loaf Pita

Just before serving, split and toast the bread and break it into pieces. Add bread to the salad bowl and toss, spooning dressing up through the salad to coat all ingredients.

NAKED CHILDREN IN THE GRASS

Does the name of this recipe give you a flash of an old-fashioned, hot summer evening, romping children, and a band playing Sousa in the park? We hope it does, for this recipe, too, belongs behind that nostalgic scrim. It's wedded to a July evening when all anyone wanted was a refreshing, but satisfying, accompaniment for buttered corn on the cob, sliced tomatoes sprinkled with fresh basil, and chunks of whole grain bread. We once heard of a Dutch recipe called "Naked Children in the Grass." We don't remember its makings, but when you prepare this one you'll see why we named it as we have.

PREPARATION TIME 20 MINUTES   SERVES 4 GENEROUSLY

   3   cups cooked garbanzos, drained
   1   small onion, sliced
  ¼   pound fresh mushrooms, sliced
   1   cup   French-cut green beans, cooked and drained
  ½   sweet green pepper, cut in thin strips
        Lebanese Salad Dressing

Combine salad ingredients, pour the dressing over, and toss to mix well. Chill until serving time.

   1   small head leaf lettuce (salad bowl, romaine, etc.), torn into bits

Place lettuce in a large salad bowl, add the garbanzo mixture and toss.

ENSALADA CON HUEVOS

The flesh of the avocado has been described as "glowing green gold." Little wonder it is reputed to have an exotic past and a glamorous reputation. But there's a totally different side to the avocado's makeup; nutritionally, it's not high in calories, high in vitamins and minerals, and without so much as a trace of cholesterol. You'll appreciate all of its virtues in this really good-looking salad.

PREPARATION TIME 5 MINUTES   SERVES 4

   1   medium head iceberg lettuce
  ½   cup chopped walnuts

Tear lettuce into salad bowl. Sprinkle nuts on lettuce.

   1   avocado

Cut the avocado in half, cutting across its middle. Twist gently to separate the halves. Remove seed, peel, and slice across to make rings. Arrange the rings on the lettuce.

   2   hard-cooked eggs, sliced

Arrange the egg·slices on and partially under, the avocado rings. Serve with Salsa Piquante (p. 105).

HOT POTATO SALAD

Obviously, this isn't a salad you'll find in the corner deli. The texture's intriguing and the seasonings provide a somewhat unusual piquancy. It's not even the potato salad that mother used to make.

PREPARATION TIME 15 MINUTES   SERVES 6
COOKING TIME 3 MINUTES
BROILING TIME 3 TO 5 MINUTES

> 6   medium potatoes
> ½   cup water

Peel potatoes and cut into ½-inch slices. Cook over water on rack in pressure cooker for 3 minutes. Mash in a broilerproof baking dish.

> 1   medium onion, chopped
> 2   hard-cooked eggs
> 4   stalks celery or 2 green peppers, chopped
> ⅓   cup vinegar
> 1½   teaspoons salt
> 1   teaspoon dry mustard
> ⅓   cup salad oil

Mix all of these with the mashed potatoes.

> **Grated cheddar cheese**

Sprinkle generously—as much as ½ pound—on top of mashed potato mixture. Broil until a pleasing brown. Serve while it's hot.

RICE SALAD MARBELLA

This splendid buffet salad is a Spanish classic. The rice mixture may be made as much as a day ahead, and it will only improve with waiting. Besides being stunning to look at, this salad is nourishing and refreshing.

PREPARATION TIME 15 MINUTES   SERVES 6 TO 8

- 3½ cups cooked brown rice
- 2 sweet green peppers, chopped
- 1 small onion, chopped
- 2 small cloves garlic, minced
- ¾ cup coarsely chopped almonds or walnuts
- 1 tablespoon chopped parsley

Combine ingredients in a large mixing bowl.

- ⅓ cup olive oil
- 3 tablespoons wine vinegar
- 1 teaspoon paprika
- ½ teaspoon salt
- ¼ teaspoon freshly ground black pepper

Put these ingredients in a small jar, cover and shake well to blend, and pour over the rice mixture. Toss until all ingredients are well mixed. Refrigerate until serving time.

- Lettuce
- 3 hard-cooked eggs, quartered
- 3 medium tomatoes, quartered
- 2 tablespoons chopped fresh basil or parsley, or other fresh herb
- Salt and pepper to taste

On a large, shallow serving platter, arrange a bed of lettuce. Mound the rice mixture in the center, smoothing it with the back of a spoon. Surround the salad with a decorative arrangement of egg and tomato wedges. Sprinkle wedges lightly with salt and pepper and scatter chopped herbs over all.

BANANA-PEANUT SALAD

We've found that this salad pleased consumers of all ages. If you have a salad problem child, this one might very well serve as a wedge in the salad door. Today, this salad. Tomorrow—who knows—maybe even raw spinach or escarole.

PREPARATION TIME 5 MINUTES   SERVES 4

    1   head iceberg lettuce

Break into chunks in 4 salad bowls.

    4   bananas
    1   cup salted peanuts
    ½   cup mung bean sprouts (optional)

Slice a banana over the lettuce in each of the bowls. Sprinkle peanuts and sprouts, if used, over the banana slices. Serve with Classic French Dressing or mayonnaise.

PEAR AND PLUM SALAD

This might be called, pear, plum, and other nuances, for this salad is a medley of sensory subtleties. For example, the cabbage almost drowns out what the nuts and crystallized ginger are trying to express. So be alert. Don't miss an enjoyable thing.

PREPARATION TIME 10 MINUTES   SERVES 6

    4   cups shredded cabbage
    6   ripe plums, cut into small chunks
    ½   cup mayonnaise
    ½   cup sour cream
    ¼   cup chopped walnuts
    3   ripe Bartlett pears, cut into small chunks and coated
        with 2 tablespoons lemon juice
    1   teaspoon salt
    2   tablespoons chopped crystallized ginger

Combine all ingredients, tossing thoroughly. Keep refrigerated until served.

PLATA DE FRUTAS

One of our favorite breakfasts, when vacationing in Mexico or the Caribbean, is a large tray of fresh fruit—luscious familiar fruit, such as ripe slices of pineapple, mango, banana, and papaya, and others that are unfamiliar, exotic, and delicious. At home, we sometimes make up our own platas de frutas, using those we're able to find in our market.

Here's a tray salad that is ideal for a festive brunch or lunch, served with cottage cheese and warm, herb-flavored whole wheat rolls. Vary the selection of fruit according to what's around.

PREPARATION TIME 20 MINUTES   **SERVES 8**

3   large bananas, cut in 1-inch diagonal slices
2   medium avocados, pitted, peeled, and sliced
     Lime juice
     Lettuce
½   medium fresh pineapple, peeled, cored, and cubed or 1 mango, peeled and sliced
2   California seedless oranges, peeled and sliced crosswise
1   cup seedless white grapes, halved
3   tablespoons chopped crystallized ginger

Dip the bananas and avocados in lime juice to prevent darkening. On a large lettuce-lined tray, arrange the various fruits, keeping each variety separate. Sprinkle the chopped ginger over the top and cover with plastic wrap. Refrigerate until serving time.

¼   cup chopped cashew nuts or almonds

Scatter nuts over the top. Serve Lime Dressing separately.

CLASSIC FRENCH DRESSING

PREPARATION TIME 2 MINUTES   MAKES ABOUT ¾ CUP

- 3 tablespoons wine vinegar or lemon juice, or a combination
- ½ cup best quality olive oil*
- ½ teaspoon dry mustard, or 1 teaspoon prepared Dijon mustard
- ½ teaspoon salt

  Freshly ground black pepper to taste

Place all ingredients in a small jar with a screw-top lid and shake vigorously. Or blend all together in a blender or food processor.

Variations: There are many delightful additions you can make to a simple French dressing. To name a few—a crushed clove of garlic, a little sesame paste (or a sprinkling of sesame seeds), herbs, parsley, sieved hard-cooked egg yolk.

LEBANESE SALAD DRESSING

PREPARATION TIME 2 MINUTES   MAKES ⅔ CUP

- ⅓ cup olive oil
- ⅓ cup lemon juice
- 1 clove garlic, crushed
- ½ teaspoon salt or more
- 5 or 6 grinds of pepper
- 4 or 5 fresh sage leaves, chopped (optional)

Combine all ingredients in a small jar with screw-top lid. Shake well. If possible, allow to stand for a short time before using.

*There is considerable variation in olive oils. The best ones, from the first pressing, are very pale in color and have a delicate flavor. They are also more expensive. Less desirable oils from second or third pressings have a strong flavor and often lead people to believe they don't like olive oil. If the best is not available, we suggest using regular salad oil for dressings, or at least diluting the cheaper variety with salad oil.

OUT-OF-SIGHT DRESSING

The name of this dressing harbors a double entendre, for—at one and the same time—it's laudatory and descriptive. Taste justifies the praise. As we proceed, just how it's descriptive will become clear. Especially recommended for a tossed green salad: different kinds of lettuce and raw spinach.

PREPARATION TIME 3 MINUTES   MAKES APPROXIMATELY ⅓ CUP

    Small clove garlic
¼ **teaspoon salt**

Dice garlic into salad bowl. Scatter salt over garlic, then mash the salted garlic with the back of a teaspoon.

¼ **cup oil**
2 **tablespoons vinegar**

Pour into the salad bowl. Stir to combine all ingredients. Refrigerate while salad is being made. Place salad over dressing and refrigerate. When you're ready to serve, toss the salad so that all of it is coated with dressing.

SALSA PIQUANTE

This dressing, as its name would have you believe, is a sauce with a sharp flavor. It certainly enlivens any salad that's in the least bland. *Viva muy piquante!*

PREPARATION TIME 5 MINUTES   MAKES APPROXIMATELY 1½ CUPS

⅓ **cup salad oil**
⅔ **cup lemon juice**
¼ **cup confectioners' sugar**
¼ **cup vinegar**
2 **teaspoons salt**
2 **teaspoons paprika**
1½ **teaspoons dry mustard**
    Pepper to taste

Blend and chill.

TOMATO-RED DRESSING

Because this dressing is so easy to make, it's advisable to make just the amount you need. (Freshly made dressing, after all, is better.) We've found that this particular dressing is liked by even the most particular among us.

PREPARATION TIME 5 MINUTES   **MAKES 1 CUP**

- ¼ cup vinegar
- ⅜ cup oil
- ½ cup catsup
- ½ teaspoon salt
  Few turns of pepper grinder
- 1 tablespoon brown sugar (optional)

Place all the ingredients in blender and blend 20 seconds at medium speed.

LIME DRESSING

PREPARATION TIME 2 MINUTES   **MAKES 1 CUP**

- ⅓ cup lime juice
- ½ cup salad oil
- 2 tablespoons rum
- 1 tablespoon honey
- ½ teaspoon ground coriander

Mix all ingredients together. If refrigerated, bring to room temperature and stir well before using.

WATERCRESS DRESSING

PREPARATION TIME 2 MINUTES   MAKES APPROXIMATELY 2 CUPS

 1   clove garlic, peeled
 ¼   teaspoon salt
 1   bunch watercress
 1   cup mayonnaise

With motor running, drop garlic into container of blender or food processor. Add salt. Divide watercress into 3 or 4 sections and add them one at a time. Blend until well chopped. Add mayonnaise, and blend until just mixed.

Breads

There are those who have the mistaken notion, to which they cling tenaciously, that breadmaking is not only an art, but an esoteric one. Riding this error piggyback is another fallacious idea: only a chosen few can bake bread successfully. We don't agree. If you can read directions and follow them—sometimes, we must admit, no easy feat—you can bake bread. Of course, after a time, through repetition, trial, error, and then success after success, you improve.

There's a reason for the present-day hunger to bake bread. It's an expression of a desire to trade the present for the past. "Homemade" does evoke the past. It also stands for purity and quality—and not for a required listing of complex chemical ingredients, dedicated to the preservation of shelf life rather than consumer life. Of course, it may be that the past was virtuous in this regard only because it hadn't had time enough to perfect sophisticated adulterants.

Baking in the home does give you control. You can have whole wheat flour milled from protein-rich hard red wheat, and white flour from which nutrients haven't been bleached. Our recipes call for such ingredients, and we've usually specified that the whole wheat flour be stone ground, because this old-fashioned process retains all the body, natural texture, and richness of the wheat berry.

In addition to wholesomeness, we've aimed at providing breads that can be made as quickly and easily as possible—sourdough breads, for example, that can be made faster than they've ever been made. And you'll also find the mixes and CoolRise recipes a great convenience.

Now, bake if you've never baked before. And if you have, enjoy these new recipes.

When Robin Hood Flour and Fleischmann's Yeast put their corporate heads together and came up with Rapidmix and CoolRise breads, they won our eternal gratitude. Rapidmix is the method of adding undissolved yeast to the dry ingredients, then adding short-ening and hot water from the tap. This method can be used with all yeast recipes.

The secret of CoolRise baking is controlled rising in the refriger-ator. This means that bread can be quickly mixed and shaped, then refrigerated for 2 to 24 hours. Using this method, we can conve-niently fill our houses with the tantalizing aroma of baking bread just before dinner, and who could ask for a better appetizer? Nearly any bread recipe can be adapted to CoolRise baking, by doubling the yeast and following the CoolRise procedure. If the recipe calls for milk, we use hot tap water, but add powdered instant dry milk to the flour.

CHAPATTI

If you need bread desperately—and are pressed for time—try chapatti, a flat bread from Northern India with a delicious whole grain flavor. They're as nourishing as they are simple. Use them as you would any bread; they wouldn't, however, be suitable for making French toast.

PREPARATION TIME 10 MINUTES   MAKES 6 OR 8 CHAPATTI
COOKING TIME 12 TO 18 MINUTES

- ½ cup cornmeal
- 1   cup whole wheat flour
- ⅛ teaspoon salt

Mix together thoroughly.

- 2   tablespoons butter

Cut the butter into the flour-cornmeal mixture. (This can be done most easily in a food processor, using the cutting blade.)

- ½ cup cold water (approximately)

Add only enough water to make the ingredients cling together in a ball. Cut this ball into 6 or 8 pieces. Flatten each piece on a floured board with the palm of the hand and then roll with a rolling pin until each piece is 5 to 6 inches in diameter. To make the pieces circular, keep turning them over between rolls of the rolling pin. Cook on a hot buttered griddle until brown areas appear, 3 to 4 minutes on each side.

Note: Other flour, bran, and cornmeal combinations: 1. 1 cup whole wheat flour, ½ cup bran. 2. 1 cup cornmeal, ¼ cup bran, ¼ cup whole wheat flour. 3. 1 cup cornmeal, ½ cup whole wheat flour. Experiment with other combinations. You might also try using milk instead of water.

HUNDRED PERCENT WHOLE WHEAT BREAD

This delicious, handsome loaf combines the Rapidmix and CoolRise methods. An additional bonus—only one bowl is used!

PREPARATION TIME 15 MINUTES
RESTING TIME 60 MINUTES
REFRIGERATION TIME 2 TO 24 HOURS   MAKES 2 LOAVES
BAKING TIME 30 TO 40 MINUTES

> 5½ to 6½ cups stone-ground whole wheat flour
> 2   packages (2 tablespoons) active dry yeast
> 1   tablespoon salt

Spoon flour into measuring cup and level off. Pour onto wax paper. Add 2 cups of the flour to the large bowl of electric mixer and stir in yeast and salt. Blend well.

> ¼ cup honey
> 3 tablespoons soft butter
> 2½ cups hot tap water (120° to 130°)

Add honey, butter, and hot water. Beat at medium speed for 2 minutes, scraping bowl occasionally. Add 1 cup more flour. Beat at high speed for 2 minutes or until thick and elastic. Gradually stir in enough of remaining flour to make a soft kneadable dough which leaves sides of bowl. Knead 5 to 8 minutes. Dough will be slightly sticky. Cover dough with plastic wrap, then a towel. Let rest 20 minutes on a board. Punch down, divide dough in half, shape into loaves and place in greased 8½-x-4½-x-2½-inch loaf pans. (Correct pan size is important for best results.)

> Cooking oil

Brush loaves lightly with oil. Cover pans loosely with plastic wrap. Let stand in a warm, draft-free place for 20 minutes. Refrigerate 2 to 24 hours. When ready to bake, remove from refrigerator. Uncover. Let stand 20 minutes while preheating oven to 400°. Puncture any surface bubbles carefully just before baking. Bake for 30 to 40 minutes until done. Use a lower oven rack for best results. Cover loosely with foil last 5 to 10 minutes if crust browns too quickly.

Remove from pan immediately. Brush top crust with butter if soft crust is desired. Cool on rack.

Variation: We often make another version of this bread that contains these ingredients:

5½ to 6½ cups unbleached white flour
2   packages (2 tablespoons) active dry yeast
⅔   cup instant nonfat dry milk
¼   cup wheat germ
¼   cup soft butter
2   cups hot tap water

The procedure is exactly the same, except that this bread doesn't require the 20 minutes resting time *after* shaping.

FAST AND EASY CRACKED WHEAT FRENCH BREAD

To the delightful crisp crust of French bread, we've added the crunch of cracked wheat. There's been a subtraction, too—of much of the time needed to prepare such a loaf of distinction. If lack of time has kept you from baking French bread, this most certainly is the recipe for you.

PREPARATION TIME 30 MINUTES   **MAKES 2 LONG LOAVES**
RISING TIME 20 MINUTES
BAKING TIME 40 MINUTES

> 1¼ cups cracked wheat
> 1 tablespoon salt
> 1½ cups boiling water

Put cracked wheat in a large mixing bowl, add salt, pour in boiling water and mix. Cool to lukewarm (110° to 115°). Speed this up by putting the mixing bowl in a larger bowl containing cold water.

> 1 tablespoon brown sugar
> ¾ cup lukewarm water
> 1 package (1 tablespoon) active dry yeast

Put sugar in water and stir. Add yeast. Stir again. When yeast has bubbled up and become foamy—in 5 to 10 minutes—and cracked wheat mixture has cooled to lukewarm, add the yeast and the water it's in to the cracked wheat mixture.

> 1½ cups whole wheat flour
> 3 cups unbleached white flour

Add the flours to the mixture, knead and make a soft dough. (Use more flour if needed.) Put the dough in a greased bowl, revolve dough to grease it. Cover. Turn the oven to warm, 150°. After 1½ minutes, turn off the oven. Put the bowl in the turned-off oven for 15 minutes.

Take dough from oven and punch it down. Divide the dough into two equal pieces. Shape each piece into a long French loaf by rolling the dough on a board and/or between your hands.

Sprinkle cornmeal on two ungreased cookie sheets. Put the loaves on the cookie sheets and let them rise for 5 minutes.

With a sharp knife make 3 or 4 diagonal slashes, ⅛-inch deep, in each loaf. Brush the loaves with cold water. Place them in the oven and turn the heat to 400°. Put a container of boiling water under the loaves. Bake 40 minutes.

Should any of the bread be left after a day or two, it makes fine toast.

SIXTY-MINUTE ROLLS

These dinner rolls can be made and baked in just 60 minutes. They are delicious while still oven-hot, when cooled a bit, or even cold. The fun of making them into different shapes must, in a small way, be related to the feelings of a sculptor at work. The consumer enjoys this variety of form, too, but this doesn't in the least slow down the eating.

PREPARATION TIME 18 MINUTES   MAKES 2 DOZEN ROLLS
RISING TIME 30 MINUTES
BAKING TIME 12 MINUTES

    3½ cups flour
    3   tablespoons sugar
    2   packages (2 tablespoons) active dry yeast
    1   teaspoon salt

Mix dry ingredients together thoroughly.

    1   cup milk
    ½   cup water
    ¼   cup butter

Heat liquids and butter in a saucepan over low heat. Butter does not need to melt, but liquid should be very warm (120° to 130°). If you don't have a thermometer, test liquid on wrist. Liquid should feel a bit more than warm, but not hot. Gradually add liquid to flour mixture and beat in an electric mixer or with a large spoon.

    1½ cups flour

Add flour until dough is no longer sticky. Use more than this amount if necessary. Knead until dough has an elastic quality. Place dough in greased bowl. Turn until bottom is greased, then turn so greased side is up. Cover, place bowl in a pan of lukewarm water and let rise for 15 minutes. Punch dough down. On a floured board, divide dough into 2 or 3 parts, depending on the number of shapes you are going to make. Shape rolls, cover, and let rise in warm oven (90°) for 15 minutes. Preheat oven to 425°.

   Bake for 12 minutes. Remove from baking sheets and cool on wire racks.

Note: The simplest shape is a ball, made by rolling a small piece of dough between the palms of the hands. Three 1-inch diameter balls, dipped in butter and placed in a muffin tin, will produce a cloverleaf roll. And you can fashion pan rolls simply by making 2-inch balls, dipping them in butter and placing them in a layer cake pan so that they touch each other. Or a 2-inch ball can be transformed into a dinner roll. With floured hands, roll the ball between the hands until it is 4 inches long and taper its ends. Bake these rolls by placing them 1 inch apart on greased cookie sheets.

THE BETTER ENGLISH MUFFIN

Build a better mousetrap, Emerson said, and the world will beat a path to your door. If that is true, we can't begin to imagine the crowds this better muffin will attract. After all, it is delectable—and easily and quickly made.

PREPARATION TIME 30 MINUTES   MAKES 14 TO 18 MUFFINS
COOKING TIME 10 MINUTES

- 1   cup milk
- 2   tablespoons brown sugar
- 1   teaspoon salt
- 3   tablespoons butter

Scald milk in a heavy saucepan and stir in sugar, salt, and butter. Cool to lukewarm.

- 1   teaspoon brown sugar
- 1¼ cups warm water (105° to 115°)
- 2   packages (2 tablespoons) active dry yeast

Stir sugar into water. Sprinkle yeast on the water and stir again. (After 5 minutes or so, the yeast will bubble and rise.)

- 2½ cups whole wheat flour
- 2¼ cups unbleached white flour
- ¼   cup wheat germ

Mix flours and wheat germ in a large bowl and gradually add the lukewarm milk mixture, then the dissolved yeast mixture. Knead until a soft dough is formed. If dough is sticky, add additional flour. (All this can be done by hand, but more easily in an electric mixer that has a dough hook.) Turn oven to warm, 150°. After 1½ minutes, turn oven off and put covered bowl containing the dough in oven for 15 minutes. Punch dough down and cut in half. Cover one half. On a board heavily sprinkled with cornmeal, press the other half to a thickness of ½ inch. Cut this pressed-out dough into circles with a 3-inch cookie cutter (or with an empty 3-inch can with top and bottom removed). Press dough trimmings together and cut again. Use up all the dough in this way. All told, you'll have 7 to 9 circles. Place them, cornmeal side down, on an ungreased cookie sheet, cover and let rise in the still warm oven while you are repeating these steps with remaining half of dough. Turn griddle to high setting, 420°, and grease lightly, only once, with butter. Place 3-inch circles on griddle and cook for 5 minutes on each side. Cool on wire racks. Before serving, split muffins in half, toast thoroughly and butter.

PITA
(The Middle Eastern bread with a pocket)

Pita is—to use the vernacular—a fun bread. After all, what bread while baking puffs up like a balloon? There's a great deal of fun, too, in stuffing it with all sorts of scrumptious fillings. Only a staid nutritionist would see only the serious side of pita bread: vitamins, minerals, dietary fiber—that sort of thing.

PREPARATION TIME 30 MINUTES   **MAKES 4**
BAKING TIME 30 MINUTES

> 1   **cup warm water, 115° (feels extra warm when tested on wrist)**
> ⅛   **teaspoon sugar**
> 1½   **packages (1½ tablespoons) active dry yeast**

Warm a bowl with hot tap water. Into this bowl stir ½ cup of the warm water with the sugar. Sprinkle yeast on water and stir again. When the yeast mixture becomes bubbly, after 7 to 10 minutes, add the remaining ½ cup warm water.

> 2   **tablespoons olive oil**
> ¾   **teaspoon salt**
> 3   **cups unbleached white flour**

Add oil, salt, and flour to the yeast mixture and knead thoroughly. (If dough hook is used, knead for 7 minutes after dough clings to hook.) Heat oven at 150° for 1½ minutes. Turn oven off. Put dough in bowl, cover and place in oven for 15 minutes. Punch dough down. (It will be warm and slightly sticky.) Knead briefly on floured board. Divide into four equal pieces. Flatten each piece with the palm of the hand. With rolling pin, rolling from the center out, form each piece into a circle 6 to 7 inches in diameter. Dust two cookie sheets with cornmeal and place two pitas on each sheet. Cover and let rest in the still warm oven for 5 minutes. Turn over carefully, bottom side up. Remove from oven. Preheat oven to 500°. Put cookie sheets, side by side, on the lowest rack in the oven for 5 minutes. Do not open oven door during this time. The pitas will puff up. Then transfer the cookie sheets to the middle rack for 3 to 5 minutes. If the pitas look pale, they may be put under the broiler for a few seconds—just long enough for them to become slightly brown. After pitas cool to lukewarm on cooling racks, wrap them in plastic to prevent them from losing their soft, pliant quality.

Variation: For a whole wheat-white pita, substitute for the 3 cups of unbleached white flour: 2 cups unbleached white flour, ¾ cup whole wheat flour, ¼ cup wheat germ. For pita fillings see Index.

Sourdough Bread

Have you ever wondered how those poor devils on Devil's Island could possibly have existed on bread and water? We've decided it must have been sourdough bread.

Sourdough bread, made the traditional way, can take 10 to 12 hours to produce. *Our* version, once you have the starter, can be ready to eat in 2½ hours.

We've strayed from tradition and added yeast to the bread recipe to cut production time. This change results in a texture somewhat lighter than the San Francisco sourdough, and the tang is not quite so pronounced, but it is delicious bread. The whole wheat starter and cracked wheat or rye give it an appetizing creamy beige color and an extra-special crunch. This bread tastes best when you tear or break pieces from the loaf rather than cut it into neat slices. As yet, science has no explanation for this phenomenon.

WHOLE WHEAT STARTER

A starter is extremely easy to make—there's no apparent witchcraft involved. Once you have your starter, it can be yours forever, improving as it is used and replenished, and can be passed on to your heirs along with the silverware and Chippendale.

PREPARATION TIME 3 MINUTES   MAKES ABOUT 1½ CUPS,
STANDING TIME 4 TO 5 DAYS   BUT VOLUME WILL INCREASE
                                          OVER A PERIOD OF TIME

    1   cup skim milk
    2   tablespoons plain low-fat yogurt

Heat milk to lukewarm (90° to 100°), and pour into a slightly warmed 1½ quart container (glass, ceramic, or plastic) with a tight-fitting lid. Stir in yogurt. Cover and let stand in a warm spot (85° to 90°) until a curd has formed and the starter has the consistency of loose yogurt—about 2 days. If a clear liquid accumulates on top, don't be disturbed.

1 cup stone-ground whole wheat flour

Stir flour into yogurt and mix well. Cover tightly and let starter stand until it is full of bubbles and has a pleasantly sour smell—2 or 3 more days. It is now ready to use or refrigerate.

Starter should be used every week or so, if possible, in order to keep it active. However, we've left ours in the refrigerator undisturbed for as long as 6 months, and it still bubbled enthusiastically after standing in a warm place for several hours. If your starter separates, just give it a stir. Starter can be frozen. After thawing, it may take 24 hours in a warm place to bring it back to life.

When you plan to use your starter, take it out of the refrigerator the night before. (Otherwise, you'll have to let it stand in a warm place for several hours until it becomes light and full of bubbles.) After removing the amount you need, put back an equal amount of flour and skim milk. For example, if you use 1 cup of starter, blend together 1 cup of warm skim milk and 1 cup of whole wheat flour and stir back into the remaining starter. Cover and let it stand in a warm place until it has bubbles, then refrigerate. Even if you're not planning to use any starter, it's a good idea to remove and discard a half cup or so every few weeks. Then replenish the starter as described.

CRACKED WHEAT SOURDOUGH

PREPARATION TIME 25 MINUTES   MAKES 3 LOAVES
RISING TIME 1 HOUR AND 20 MINUTES
BAKING TIME 35 MINUTES

    1   **cup boiling water**
    ½   **cup cracked wheat (or cracked rye)** *

Pour boiling water over cracked wheat and set aside until cooled to lukewarm. Place container in pan of cold water and stir frequently to speed cooling.

    ½   **cup warm water (about 110°)**
    1   **package (1 tablespoon) active dry yeast**
    2   **teaspoons sugar**

Pour water into a large mixing bowl. Sprinkle in dry yeast and allow to stand a minute or two. Add sugar and stir.

    1   **cup sourdough starter**
    2   **teaspoons salt**
    3   **cups unbleached all-purpose flour**

Blend starter, salt, and flour into the yeast mixture. Add the cooled cracked wheat, including any soaking water that has not been absorbed. Mix dough well. It will be a rough mass, and rather sticky. Cover bowl with plastic wrap and place in an oven that has been set at 150° for 3 minutes and then turned off. Allow dough to rise until it has doubled in volume and is light and full of bubbles, 45 to 50 minutes.

    1½ to 2 cups unbleached white flour (approximately)

Stir in enough additional flour to make a stiff dough and knead until smooth and elastic, about 10 minutes. Divide dough into 3 parts. Shape each part into a smooth cylinder. Place the loaves, spaced well apart, on a large baking sheet that has been liberally sprinkled with cornmeal on the areas where the bread will rest. Cover the shaped loaves with a kitchen towel that has been lightly dusted with flour. Top with a sheet of plastic wrap. Place the loaves in the turned-off oven to rise until nearly doubled and puffy looking, 30 to 40 minutes. Remove from oven.

---

* You can crack whole grain wheat or rye in your blender or grain mill.

Preheat the oven to 400°. Just before the bread is placed in the oven, make a long, lengthwise slash, about ½-inch deep, in the top of each loaf, using a sharp knife or razor blade. Place a large shallow pan (broiler pan is fine) on the lowest oven shelf and pour boiling water into it to a depth of ¼ inch. Brush loaves of bread with water and place them in the oven. Bake about 25 minutes, or until loaves sound hollow when tapped on the bottom. Cool on racks—or stand loaves on end, leaning against a support so the air can circulate freely around them. Sourdough bread is best if reheated in the oven before serving.

Variations: Sourdough starter can be made with unbleached all-purpose flour. Whole milk may be substituted for skim milk, but the flavor will be less sour. Cracked rye makes an excellent substitute for the cracked wheat.

SOURDOUGH ROLLS

After the dough has been kneaded, roll it into a rectangle and cut into 18 pieces (or more or fewer pieces, according to the size you'd like your rolls to be). Shape each piece into a smooth ball or oblong and arrange on cornmeal-sprinkled baking sheets, spaced several inches apart. Cover and let rise as previously indicated. Make one slash in each roll, spray or brush with cold water and bake at 400° about 20 minutes. If using 2 baking sheets, switch them at the midpoint of the baking time. Cool on racks.

SOURDOUGH POCKET BREAD

After kneading, divide dough into 16 parts and shape each part into a smooth ball by holding the piece of dough in the cupped palm of one hand and folding the edges inward toward the center with the other. On a lightly floured surface, flatten the ball into a circle and roll from the center outward with a rolling pin to a diameter of 6 or 7 inches. Place the circles of dough on lightly floured cloth-covered baking sheets. Cover with flour-dusted cloth, topped with a sheet of plastic wrap. Allow to rise in a turned-off oven about 30 minutes, until slightly puffy-looking. Slide the cloths off the baking sheets onto a counter, with the dough circles still on them, being careful not to deflate the loaves. Dust the baking sheets with cornmeal and place dough circles on them with the top sides down. Handle dough circles lightly so they do not deflate. Bake only one sheet of dough circles at a time. Preheat the oven to 500°. Place the baking sheet on the lowest rack and bake for 4 to 5 minutes. Loaves will puff up like pillows and still be pale in color. To brown them, switch oven to broil and place pan of bread 4 inches from broiler unit for about 1 minute. Watch carefully. Remove from oven, wrap loosely in a kitchen towel. They will deflate somewhat as they cool. If not to be served at once, package in sealed plastic bags and refrigerate or freeze. To reheat, wrap loosely in foil, place in cold oven, set temperature at 400° and heat 8 to 10 minutes. If frozen, place in cold oven, set at 450° and heat 15 to 20 minutes.

SOURDOUGH PIZZA

Sourdough makes unusually crisp, delicious pizza crust. After kneading the dough, divide it into two pieces and gently pull, pat, and stretch each to fit a 14-inch pizza pan that has been lightly oiled and sprinkled with cornmeal. Do not allow the dough to rise again. Place pans in a 500° oven and bake 10 minutes, switching pan positions midway. Remove from the oven, brush dough with olive oil and add tomato sauce and your favorite toppings. Continue baking at 500° for about 15 minutes, again switching pan positions at the halfway point, until toppings are hot and bubbling and crust is a crisp golden brown.

BASIC BREAD MIX

Thank heavens, the Israelites weren't prudent enough to have a bread mix on hand before they had to hurry out of Egypt. Otherwise, we might never have known about matzos.

Here's a bread mix you can make yourself, and it will give you a real psychological boost to have it waiting on the shelf, all ready for the yeast and liquid ingredients. Stored in large, tightly closed canisters or in heavy plastic bags, the dry mixture will keep on the kitchen shelf for many weeks. You may, if you wish, use all whole wheat flour instead of whole wheat and white, but if you do, expect a smaller loaf. In warm weather, keep the mix in a cool place or refrigerated, unless you plan to use it up quickly.

PREPARATION TIME 10 MINUTES   MAKES 22 CUPS OF MIX,
                               ENOUGH FOR 8 LOAVES OF BREAD

- 12 cups unbleached white flour
- 8   cups stone-ground whole wheat flour
- 2   cups instant dry milk powder
- ¾   cup sugar
- 4   tablespoons salt

Divide ingredients in half and mix in two batches in large bowl of electric mixer on slow speed (or by hand in a large bowl with a wire whisk or big spoon).

Stir or shake mix well each time you use it before measuring amount. If it has been refrigerated, bring to room temperature before using (page 275).

WHOLE WHEAT BISCUITS

Metaphorically, biscuits are pinch hitters; they may be called upon when a meal's prospects look bleak. These biscuits—hot and crunchy—can brighten breakfast, lunch, or dinner. And they can be made with not much more effort than it takes to put napkins on the table.

PREPARATION TIME 5 MINUTES   **MAKES 10 TO 13 BISCUITS**
BAKING TIME ABOUT 15 MINUTES

> 2   cups whole wheat flour
> 4   teaspoons baking powder
> 1   teaspoon salt
> ½   cup instant dry milk

Mix together thoroughly in the bowl of an electric mixer.

> ⅓   cup oil
> ⅔   cup water

Combine oil and water and pour into dry ingredients. Stir just enough to moisten them. On a lightly floured board, knead dough briefly, merely folding it over a few times. Preheat the oven to 400°. Press the dough with your hands to a uniform ½-inch thickness. With a biscuit cutter, or a glass having a diameter of 2½ inches, cut the dough into thick circles. Place them on an ungreased cookie sheet and bake for about 15 minutes until they're light brown.

SHORTCUT DOUGH

An excellent all-round bread dough, good for sandwiches, toast, rolls, and even pizza.

PREPARATION TIME 15 MINUTES   MAKES 2 LOAVES
RISING TIME 30 TO 40 MINUTES
BAKING TIME 35 TO 40 MINUTES

> **4 tablespoons butter**

Remove butter from refrigerator and place in warm spot to soften.

> **3 cups Basic Bread Mix**
> **2 packages (2 tablespoons) active dry yeast**
> **2 cups hot tap water (120° to 130°)**

In large bowl of electric mixer, stir the yeast and bread mix together. Add the softened butter to the hot tap water and stir to melt the butter. Gradually add the liquid to the dry ingredients and beat, first on low speed, then increasing to medium speed for 2 minutes. Scrape the bowl occasionally. Increase speed to high and beat for 2 more minutes.

> **2½ cups Basic Bread Mix**
> **Additional flour**

Beat in bread mix and enough additional flour to make a soft dough that cleans the sides of the bowl. Turn onto a floured board and knead for 5 minutes or until smooth and elastic.

Shape dough into a ball and return to the bowl. Cover bowl and place in oven that has been set at 150° for 3 minutes and then turned off. Allow dough to rise 15 to 20 minutes. Punch dough down and divide into two equal pieces. Shape each piece into a loaf and place in two well-greased 8½ x 4½ x 2½-inch bread pans. Cover loaves with a towel, topped with a sheet of plastic wrap. Place pans in the warm oven. Let loaves rise 15 to 20 minutes or until the crest of the loaf is ¾ inch above the rim of the pan. Remove the covering from the loaves, leaving them in the oven, and turn the setting to 400°. Bake 35 to 40 minutes or until the loaves sound hollow when tapped on the bottom and crusts are nicely browned.

Cracked Wheat Variation: To make cracked wheat bread, pour 1 cup of boiling water over ½ cup cracked wheat, cover and allow to stand 20 minutes, stirring occasionally. Proceed as in Shortcut Dough recipe, using only 1⅓ cups hot tap water. Beat in cracked wheat after liquid and dry ingredients have been well mixed together.

Pizza Variation: To make two 12-inch pizzas, cut the bread recipe in half and increase the hot water to 1¼ cups. Don't let the dough rise after placing in greased pizza pans. Bake at 450° for about 10 minutes, switching pan positions after the first half of the baking time. Spread with your favorite topping and return to the oven for about 10 minutes more, again switching pans halfway.

THE 15-MINUTE SUPER-BISCUIT

Super, of course, denotes an extravaganza of virtues. However, this prefix has been used so indiscriminately that it has virtually become meaningless. We've therefore been hesitant about calling this biscuit a super-biscuit, but that's what it really is. And having a mix for it makes it even more super.

To prepare the mix:

PREPARATION TIME 5 MINUTES   MAKES 5 CUPS OF MIX

- 2 cups whole wheat flour
- 1 cup cornmeal
- 1 cup rye flour
- ½ cup soy flour
- ¼ cup brown sugar
- 3½ teaspoons baking powder
- 1¾ teaspoons baking soda
- 1¾ teaspoons salt

Mix ingredients thoroughly. Store where it's cool and dry.

To prepare biscuits:

PREPARATION TIME 5 MINUTES   MAKES 8 BISCUITS
BAKING TIME 10 MINUTES

- 2 cups Super-Biscuit mix
- ½ cup milk
- 2 tablespoons oil

Pour mix into a bowl, add milk and oil and blend thoroughly. Shape into a ball of dough and divide it into 8 equal parts. Make a ball of each part by rolling it between your hands. Place one of the balls in the palm of one hand and slap it a few times with the palm of the other hand. This will form a perfectly round piece of dough; it should be approximately ½-inch thick and have a diameter of about 2½ inches. Shape all 8 pieces in this way. Bake each side 5 minutes on a lightly greased griddle, set at high temperature.

BUTTERNUT MUFFINS

These muffins are adapted from an old, longtime favorite recipe that called for pumpkin. We've found that butternut squash (the pear-shaped one with a tan or pinkish tan skin) has a richer flavor and color and is a more convenient size. When it's available, we use it instead of pumpkin. A quick and easy way to cook any winter squash is to cut it, unpeeled, into quarters (or more pieces if very large), scoop out the seeds and stringy part, and steam it over boiling water until tender when pierced with a fork, about 7 to 10 minutes. The skin will peel off easily and the pulp is ready for mashing. Try Butternut Muffins with mulled cider or herbal tea.

PREPARATION TIME 7 MINUTES   **MAKES 1 DOZEN MUFFINS**
BAKING TIME 30 MINUTES

Preheat oven to 425°.

- ¾ cup milk
- 2 tablespoons butter

Heat milk and butter together until milk is warm and butter is softened.

- 1 cup cooked, mashed butternut squash
- 1 egg

Beat squash and egg into the milk mixture.

- 1½ cups unbleached white flour
- 1 teaspoon salt
- 1 tablespoon baking powder
- ¼ teaspoon cinnamon
- ¼ teaspoon ground ginger
  Pinch of ground cloves

Sift dry ingredients into a large bowl.

- ¼ cup chopped nuts
- ¼ cup raisins

Stir nuts and raisins into dry ingredients. Make a well in the center of dry mixture and pour milk and squash mixture into it all at once. Stir only long enough to moisten all ingredients. Spoon batter into well-greased, medium-sized muffin tin, filling cups ⅔ full. Bake at 425° until tops are rounded and lightly browned. Remove from pan and serve.

SUNFLOWER DINNER MUFFINS

Because of their sweet nature, muffins usually wind up on the breakfast or tea table. Nonsweet muffins, though, can fit in nicely at dinner—they're especially good with hearty soups. These coarse-textured muffins have a nutlike flavor and are similar to the ones Grandmother used to make. She called them "gems"—and that's just what they are.

PREPARATION TIME 7 MINUTES   MAKES 1 DOZEN MUFFINS
BAKING TIME 25 MINUTES

Preheat oven to 375°.

- 1   egg
- ¼   cup vegetable oil
- ¼   cup brown sugar (firmly packed)
- 1   cup milk

Beat ingredients together in a bowl until well mixed.

- 1   cup sifted unbleached white flour
- 1   cup unsifted whole wheat flour
- 1   tablespoon baking powder
- ½   teaspoon salt
- ½   cup sunflower seeds

Combine these dry ingredients in a large mixing bowl and make a well in the center. Pour egg mixture into the well all at once, and stir gently until ingredients are just moistened. Fill well-greased 2½-inch muffin cups ⅔ full with batter. Bake at 375° about 25 minutes, or until tops are rounded and lightly browned. Serve at once.

APPLE CORIANDER MUFFINS

The only thing you have to watch out for in making muffins is that you don't work too hard. The liquid ingredients should be mixed into the dry only until barely combined—about 10 or 12 stirs. If you are too zealous with your mixing, you'll end up with muffins that have tough, pale, cone-shaped crowns and interiors that are riddled with tunnels. If it's perfection you're after—take it easy!

PREPARATION TIME 7 MINUTES   MAKES 1 DOZEN MUFFINS
BAKING TIME 25 MINUTES

Preheat oven to 375°.

- ¼ cup butter
- 6 tablespoons brown sugar (firmly packed)
- 1 egg
- ½ cup milk
- ½ cup coarsely grated, peeled apple

Cream butter and sugar together until well mixed and fluffy. Beat in egg and milk and blend well. Stir in apple.

- 1¼ cups unbleached white flour
- 3 tablespoons wheat germ
- 2 teaspoons baking powder
- ¼ teaspoon ground coriander
- 1 teaspoon cinnamon
- ½ cup chopped walnuts

Blend dry ingredients together in a large mixing bowl, stirring in walnuts last. Make a well in the center, and pour wet ingredients into it all at once. Stir just until dry mixture is no longer visible. Spoon batter into a greased muffin pan, filling cups ⅔ full. Bake at 375° until lightly browned, about 25 minutes. Remove at once from pan and serve. If muffins are allowed to cool, reheat them in a tightly closed paper bag at 350° for about 5 minutes.

EASY POPOVERS

Children—and some adults—enjoy watching the progress of popovers through the glass in the oven door. Popovers do rise dramatically. Always the comedienne, Jane once cried out in horror, "They're getting bigger and bigger! They're going to take over the world!" In a somewhat different mood, Jane enjoys eating popovers, after methodically filling the holes in their insides with preserves and yogurt.

PREPARATION TIME 5 MINUTES   MAKES 8 POPOVERS USING
BAKING TIME 25 MINUTES   5-OUNCE MUFFIN CUPS

¾   cup plus 2 tablespoons milk
2   eggs
1   tablespoon oil
¾   cup sifted unbleached white flour
¼   cup wheat germ
¼   teaspoon salt

Preheat oven to 425°. Grease the cups of a muffin pan. Put all ingredients in blender and blend until smooth, about 15 seconds. Pour equal amounts into muffin cups. Bake 25 minutes, or until brown and crisp. Remove popovers from pans and puncture them to let trapped steam escape. Serve immediately. (Popovers can be reheated. Place them in a brown paper bag in a 425° oven for 5 minutes.)

1-2-3 SOY MUFFINS

A muffin that manages to be both very nourishing and quite delicious. It can also be made in 1, 2, 3 fashion: 1. Assemble dry ingredients. 2. Assemble liquid ingredients. 3. Combine dry and liquid ingredients. Producing these muffins is really as simple as that.

PREPARATION TIME 10 MINUTES MAKES 12 MUFFINS
BAKING TIME 12 MINUTES

- ½ cup sifted soy flour
- 1 cup whole wheat flour
- ¼ cup unbleached white flour
- ¼ cup wheat germ
- 1 tablespoon baking powder
- 1 teaspoon salt
- ¼ cup sunflower seeds
- ½ cup raisins

Combine thoroughly, in an electric mixer if possible.

- 1 egg
- 3 tablespoons oil
- 2 tablespoons honey (measure honey in spoon used for oil)
- 1 cup milk

Beat the egg with the oil, honey, and milk. Stir this mixture into the dry ingredients only enough to moisten them. Spoon into oiled muffin tins. Bake 12 minutes at 425°. The muffins will have a pale crown; other than that, they'll be beautifully brown.

ALWAYS READY BRAN MUFFINS

Muffins for breakfast. The phrase conjures up all sorts of pleasing sensory images. However, there's a catch—how to make the thought of muffins a reality, quickly and without too much work. This bran muffin batter, which keeps in the refrigerator for several weeks, is the glorious answer.

PREPARATION TIME 7 MINUTES   MAKES 2 TO 2½ DOZEN MUFFINS
BAKING TIME 20 MINUTES

- 3 cups unprocessed bran
- 1 cup boiling water

Mix bran and water. Cool.

- 2 eggs
- 2 cups buttermilk
- ½ cup oil
- 1 cup raisins

Add to the bran-water mixture and combine thoroughly.

- 2½ teaspoons baking soda
- ½ teaspoon salt
- ⅔ cup sugar
- 2½ cups whole wheat flour

Blend these dry ingredients, then stir into the other mixture. The batter may be used immediately or kept in the refrigerator for future use. Before using, stir batter to distribute raisins. Fill well-greased muffin tins ¾ full. Bake in 425° oven for 20 minutes. (Optional: sprinkle each muffin before baking with chopped walnuts.)

THE NONPAREIL CORN BREAD

Technically, a quick bread is one that uses a leavening agent other than yeast. Since this one uses baking powder, it is, officially, a quick bread. We heard it praised in this oblique way, "It's real good. You hardly know it's corn bread."

PREPARATION TIME 10 MINUTES   MAKES 12 TO 16 PIECES
BAKING TIME 30 MINUTES

- 1 cup unbleached white flour
- ¼ cup whole wheat flour
- ¼ cup wheat germ
- 1½ cups cornmeal
- 1 tablespoon baking powder
- ⅛ teaspoon salt

Mix these dry ingredients thoroughly and set aside.

- ½ cup brown sugar (not packed)
- ½ cup oil
- 2 eggs

Blend sugar and oil in electric mixer. Add eggs one at a time, and blend them with the sugar and oil mixture.

- 1 cup milk

Alternate stirring a little of the milk and a little of the dry ingredients into the sugar, oil, and egg mixture. Pour the batter into an oiled and floured 8-inch square pan. Bake at 400° for 30 minutes. Cool in pan. Cut into pieces and cool them on a rack.

COFFEE CAN BREAD

This bread requires no kneading and only one rising; it has a light, fine texture and a tantalizing aroma of ginger and herbs. You might think that's about all you could ask of a loaf of bread—but this bread offers more. You make it in 1-pound coffee cans (or other cans of similar size and shape) equipped with plastic lids. The dough is packed into the cans to the halfway mark and the lids snapped in place. When the dough rises to the top of the can, it flips its lid and you know it's time to bake! When you do, a big, puffy crust mushrooms out of the top of the can and there's usually a scramble to see who gets to eat it. After the "mushroom" is lopped off, the can makes a convenient container for storing the rest of the loaf, or for shipping it off to some hungry young person away at school.

PREPARATION TIME 20 MINUTES   MAKES 2 LOAVES
RISING TIME 35 TO 45 MINUTES
BAKING TIME 45 TO 55 MINUTES

> 1⅓ packages (4 teaspoons) active dry yeast
> ½   cup warm water
>   Pinch of sugar

In a large mixing bowl, sprinkle yeast over warm water, add sugar and stir to dissolve yeast. Place bowl in a warm spot until mixture foams, about 15 minutes.

> 1½ cups milk
> ¼   cup (½ stick) butter cut in 4 pieces
> 3   tablespoons honey
> 1   teaspoon grated fresh ginger or ¼ teaspoon ground ginger
> 1   teaspoon chopped fresh dill or ¼ teaspoon dried dill-weed
> ¼   teaspoon dried basil
> ¼   teaspoon dried oregano
> ¼   teaspoon dried thyme
> 1   teaspoon salt

While yeast is standing, scald the milk and stir in remaining ingredients. Cool mixture to lukewarm. Pour into the yeast and mix well.

1½ cups stone-ground whole wheat flour
3   cups unbleached white flour (approximately)

Beat flour into the liquid ingredients, one cup at a time, beating very well after each addition. (Use an electric mixer if possible.) Use all the whole wheat flour first, then add the white until batter forms a dough that will hold together in a ball but is too sticky to knead. Divid dough in half and pack each half into a *well-greased* one-pound coffee can. Press dough down firmly with greased knuckles to make sure there are no air pockets. Cover with *well-greased* plastic lids. (At this point, dough may be frozen for several weeks.)

Set cans in a warm spot until the dough rises and bursts out of the tops of the cans, carrying the lids with it. Near end of rising time, preheat oven to 350°. (Frozen dough should be allowed to stand at room temperature until the lid pops off, usually 4 or 5 hours.) Remove lids if they are still clinging to the tops of the dough, and bake the loaves in the preheated oven until puffy crown is well browned—45 to 55 minutes. Loosen crust around top edge with a thin knife, and slide loaves from the cans. Cool on a rack in upright position.

FAINT
(A quick, nut-raisin bread)

One of our children—time has obscured which one—christened this bread "Faint." Why? Julie, who claims credit for the name, explained that the bread was so good it made you feel as if you were going to faint. At any rate, this is the legend.

PREPARATION TIME 15 MINUTES   **MAKES 2 LOAVES**
BAKING TIME 45 MINUTES

Preheat oven to 350°

½   cup oil
1   cup brown sugar (not packed)

Mix shortening and sugar thoroughly.

2   eggs
1   cup milk

Add to creamed mixture and set aside.

3   cups whole wheat flour
4   teaspoons baking powder
½   teaspoon salt
1   cup coarsely chopped walnuts
1   cup raisins

Mix these dry ingredients thoroughly, and combine with reserved mixture. Spoon equal amounts into 2 buttered pans, 8½ x 4½ inches. (For a higher loaf, use an even smaller pan, 7¼ x 3½ inches.) Smooth surface with a spatula. Bake 45 minutes. Remove from pans and cool on rack.

Main Dishes

To the average person, dinner means a main dish of meat, poultry, or fish. All the rest is supporting cast. A vegetable is something lightly dismissed.

In the vegetarian cuisine, vegetables surface into main roles. One vegetable may occupy center stage, but more commonly two or three will play complementary roles, each balanced against the other for taste, texture, color, and nutrition. Many of our recipes aren't even primarily vegetable. There are legumes, grains, fruits, seeds, nuts, and cheeses wedded to the vegetables. Pita bread, sprouts, pastas, and flaky crusts also become part of the picture. Herbs and spices play an emerging role in creating an awareness of the superb range of tantalizing flavors and aromas that many people seldom, if ever, experience. The Japanese call it *awahree*. It is a new awareness of what the eating experience can be.

We've roamed the globe for recipes—China, Mexico, Rumania, Arkansas—hoping to make them distinctive and exciting, and a stimulant to your eating pleasure. Because we have also been intent on finding the easiest and quickest route to good results, we've included many top-of-the-range dishes and made frequent use of previously cooked staples as part of the recipes. However, given the choice, we have never sacrificed quality for speed.

BEAN SNAP

This is an old family favorite, and we always serve it with mashed potatoes or Hot Potato Salad. Rice is good too, but would probably be greeted with shouts of horror at our table. Tradition!

PREPARATION TIME 5 MINUTES   SERVES 4 TO 6
COOKING TIME 30 MINUTES

- 2 large onions, sliced
- 2 tablespoons butter or oil
- ½ teaspoon sugar (optional)

Sauté the onions over moderate heat in a large, heavy saucepan until soft and a nice golden brown—about 10 minutes. Sprinkle sugar over the onions while they're browning, if you wish, to caramelize them and give a deeper color.

- 1 16-ounce can tomatoes (tomatoes canned in tomato purée are best, but others may be used)
- 1 tablespoon chopped fresh basil or 1 teaspoon dried
  Salt and pepper to taste

Stir these ingredients into the onions and cook for a minute or two.

- 1½ pounds fresh green beans, ends removed and beans snapped in half
- 1 cup cooked garbanzos, drained

Add these ingredients to the saucepan, cover and simmer until beans are tender, about 20 minutes.

Menu Suggestion: Because this dish is low in protein, you might serve a tossed salad with it containing cubes of cheese, or close the meal with a high-protein dessert like Cheesecake Superstar.

ARTICHOKE SPECIAL

The artichoke has always been associated with luxury and elegance. Actually the flower bud of a thistle, it's a natural "show-off" vegetable and, as such, is an ideal choice for the special dinners of your life. The most attractive way to prepare artichokes is to stuff them. This is hardly child's play, however, and because we're dedicated to living a life of ease, we usually prepare them this carefree way, using the frozen artichoke hearts or bottoms that we find at the supermarket. See page 30 for a discussion of artichokes.

PREPARATION TIME 15 MINUTES   SERVES 4
BAKING TIME 20 MINUTES

Preheat oven to 350°.

> 2   **9-ounce packages frozen artichoke hearts, or bottoms if available**

Thaw artichokes by running water over them until they separate. Arrange them in the bottom of a shallow, greased casserole.

> 2   **tablespoons butter**
> 2   **green onions (scallions), minced**
> 1   **cup chopped fresh mushrooms**
> 1   **clove garlic, minced**

Melt butter in a large, heavy skillet and sauté onions briefly. Add mushrooms and garlic and sauté about 5 minutes.

> 1   **cup grated mild cheese**
> ½   **cup fresh bread crumbs**
> ½   **teaspoon salt**
> ¼   **teaspoon basil**
>   **Few turns of pepper grinder**

Stir ingredients into the onion-mushroom mixture.

> 2   **eggs, beaten**
> ½   **cup sour cream**

Stir eggs and sour cream together and add to mixture in skillet. Spread this mixture evenly over the artichoke hearts.

¼   cup fresh bread crumbs
¼   cup grated mild cheese
2   tablespoons melted butter

Mix crumbs and cheese and sprinkle over the top of the casserole. Drizzle with melted butter. Bake at 350°, uncovered, or until artichoke hearts are tender when pierced and top of casserole is brown and bubbling.

Note: If you happen to have some prepared, parboiled artichokes on hand (page 30), you can use the mushroom mixture as a stuffing. Fill the cavities, sprinkle tops with cheese and crumbs, dot with butter. Place in a pan, pour a small amount of boiling water in the bottom of the pan, cover tightly with foil and bake at 350° for 20 minutes or until artichokes are tender. Uncover and continue baking 5 more minutes until topping is brown and lightly crisped.

BLACK BEANS AND RICE

If you should ask our Tim what he'd like for dinner, you'd nearly always get the same answer: "Black beans and rice." Black beans are meaty and flavorful, and with rice they provide complementary nutrients.

Thick, dark, and spicy, this is a quick version of a festive South American dish called "Feijoada." If you don't already know how that's pronounced, it's "fay-*zshwah*-dah."

PREPARATION TIME 10 MINUTES   SERVES 4
COOKING TIME 30 MINUTES

   3 tablespoons cooking oil
   1 medium onion, chopped
   2 sweet green or red peppers or 1 of each, seeded and diced
   2 cloves garlic, minced

In a large, heavy saucepan, heat the oil over moderate heat. Add onion and sauté, stirring occasionally, about 3 minutes. Add peppers and garlic and cook 3 minutes longer.

   2 teaspoons ground cumin
   1 teaspoon crushed oregano

Add cumin and oregano and cook briefly, stirring.

   3 cups cooked black beans, drained
   1 tablespoon lemon juice
   1 tablespoon frozen orange juice concentrate
   2 medium tomatoes, chopped
      Salt and pepper to taste

Stir these ingredients into the sautéed mixture and simmer, covered, 5 minutes, adding a small amount of stock, water or tomato juice if needed to thin the mixture to desired consistency.

   2 tablespoons dark rum
   3 cups cooked brown rice

Mix 1 cup of the bean mixture with rum and mash to a paste with the back of a fork (or blend in blender or food processor). Add the puree to the pot set over low heat, cover and simmer about 20 minutes. Serve over hot, cooked brown rice.

Serving suggestion: If you enjoy pungent food, stir some chopped onion and chopped green chiles, a little lemon juice and a chopped tomato into the rice before serving. Sliced bananas on the side will help put out the fire.

BROCCOLI WITH CHEESE AND WATER CHESTNUTS

We usually prefer to use fresh broccoli, but in this casserole, frozen broccoli can be used successfully and it requires no precooking. If you want to use fresh broccoli, steam it covered over boiling salted water for about 5 minutes, or until barely fork tender. Allow it to cool a little, then chop it and add to the egg mixture.

PREPARATION TIME 6 MINUTES   SERVES 6 TO 8
BAKING TIME 30 MINUTES

2	eggs
1	cup cottage cheese
1	cup shredded mild cheddar cheese
3	tablespoons flour
1	teaspoon salt
¼	teaspoon dried minced onion
2	tablespoons yogurt
2	10-ounce packages frozen chopped broccoli, thawed
1	8¼-ounce can water chestnuts, drained and sliced

Beat eggs slightly in a mixing bowl with a fork or whisk. Stir in remaining ingredients. Pour into a greased, 9-inch baking dish.

Paprika

Sprinkle with paprika and bake at 350° for 30 minutes, or until firm. Cut into slices to serve.

CLASSY BROCCOLI

One usually doesn't think of broccoli and upward mobility in the same thought. We did, however, as the name of this recipe suggests. Here, made on top of the range, we have broccoli in the company of almonds—and a rich cheese sauce. Only in America!

PREPARATION TIME 10 MINUTES   SERVES 4
COOKING TIME 15 MINUTES

> 1   large onion, chopped
> 2   tablespoons butter

Sauté onions in butter for 5 minutes.

> 2   cups coarsely chopped fresh broccoli

Add to sautéed onions and stir-fry until broccoli is cooked, but still crisp.

> 1   tablespoon butter
> 1   tablespoon whole wheat flour
> ¼   teaspoon salt
>   Several turns of pepper grinder
>   Pinch crushed tarragon
> 1   cup very hot milk

Put above ingredients in blender. Start blending at low speed. Quickly change to high speed and blend for 20 seconds.

> ¾   cup diced cheddar cheese

Add cheese while blender is running at full speed. Blend for 20 seconds. Pour contents of blender into heavy saucepan and cook 3 minutes, stirring occasionally. Pour cheese sauce over broccoli and onions, then mix them together.

> Sliced almonds

Use generously to garnish individual servings.

ELEGANT LIMA BEANS

Though this is an elegant dish, a leftover and a stockpile item (see Prefab Cooking, first 3 paragraphs), can be used in its preparation. And if you use them, this dish is heated rather than cooked. The use of a casserole is merely to give these elegant lima beans an appropriate setting.

PREPARATION TIME 7 MINUTES   SERVES 4 TO 6
COOKING TIME NEEDED TO HEAT BEANS AND SAUCE

> **4** cups cooked dried lima beans (stockpile item)
> **2** cups leftover tomato sauce

Bring to boil. Remove from heat.

> **1** cup grated Swiss cheese or slices torn in bits
> **1** cup coarsely chopped walnuts
> **¼** teaspoon basil
> **1** green pepper, seeded and diced
> Toasted wheat germ

Mix all ingredients except wheat germ with hot beans and sauce. Add wheat germ a little at a time until mixture is thickened to your liking. Spoon into casserole.

> **Minced parsley**

Garnish casserole with parsley and serve.

CABBAGE À LA FRENCH CUISINE

Essentially, this is cooked cabbage, enlivened by a cheese sauce and fortified by and decorated with kidney beans. You will find—to your surprise and delight—that these mundane elements combine to produce an altogether delicious dish.

PREPARATION TIME 10 MINUTES   SERVES 4
COOKING TIME 20 MINUTES

1   medium head of cabbage, shredded

Steam cabbage until tender, about 5 minutes. Set aside, covered.

1   medium onion, chopped
¼   cup oil or butter

Sauté onion for 5 minutes.

3   tablespoons whole wheat flour
1   teaspoon salt
Freshly ground black pepper to taste
⅛   teaspoon nutmeg
½   teaspoon caraway seeds
2   cups milk
1¼   cups grated Swiss cheese

Stir flour and seasonings into the sautéed onion. Continue stirring as you gradually add milk. Cook on low heat for about 10 minutes. Remove from heat and add cheese and reserved cabbage.

2   cups cooked kidney beans, heated and drained

When serving, top cabbage with kidney beans.

CAULIFLOWER AND LEEKS À LA CRÈME

Leeks are a member of the lily family—the same one to which garlic and tulips belong. They're really a superb vegetable and are becoming much less rare in our markets. They're still expensive, but a few large ones can go a long way, as they do in this recipe.

PREPARATION TIME 10 MINUTES   SERVES 4 TO 6
COOKING TIME 20 MINUTES

> 1   small head cauliflower
> 1 or 2 large leeks

Wash cauliflower and break into flowerets. Cut off tops of leeks just above the white part and trim off the roots. Slash through the upper section lengthwise, toward but not through the bottom. Fan out leaves and wash under cold running water, making sure to clean out all grit and sand. Place cauliflower and leeks in steamer basket over ½ cup of boiling water, cover and steam about 7 minutes, or until fork tender.

> 2   cups broad noodles
> 1   tablespoon butter

While vegetables are steaming, cook noodles according to package directions. Drain, toss with butter and keep warm.

> 2   tablespoons butter
> 2   tablespoons flour
> 1½ cups milk
> ⅓   cup heavy cream
> ⅓   cup grated Parmesan cheese
>   Salt and pepper
> ½   teaspoon thyme
> 2   tablespoons minced parsley

Melt the butter in the bottom of a heatproof serving dish until it is foamy. Stir in the flour and cook, stirring with a wire whisk for a minute or two. (If you have frozen roux wafers (page 38) on hand, simply heat two of them until bubbly.) Slowly whisk in the milk, then add the cream and cheese. Cook, stirring for 1 minute. Season with salt, pepper, and thyme.

Separate the leeks into individual leaves, and add them along with the cauliflowerets to the serving dish. Toss to coat with the hot sauce. Stir in the hot drained noodles, sprinkle with parsley, and toss all together over moderate heat for a moment or two until piping hot. Serve.

CABBAGE AND MUSHROOMS

You might think East is East and West is West and never the twain, etc., but the rich, woodsy flavor of imported dried mushrooms, stir-fried with succulent cabbage and water chestnuts, then mixed with egg noodles, is an East-West combo that works. This is a satisfying dish, but light enough so that you might consider a substantial dessert such as Dark and Handsome chocolate cake or Peach Delight to round out the menu.

PREPARATION TIME 15 MINUTES   SERVES 6
COOKING TIME 6 MINUTES

    1 ounce imported dried mushrooms

Rinse mushrooms and cover with hot tap water. Allow to soak 15 minutes, drain, squeezing out liquid, and reserve soaking water. Slice mushrooms.

    2 cups medium egg noodles
    2 tablespoons butter

While mushrooms are soaking, cook noodles according to package directions, drain, stir in butter and keep warm.

    2 tablespoons butter
    1 small head cabbage, shredded
    1 8¼-ounce can water chestnuts, drained and sliced
       Salt

In a large, heavy saucepan, or wok, melt butter over moderately high heat. Add mushrooms and stir-fry for 2 minutes. Stir in cabbage and water chestnuts and salt to taste. Add ¼ cup of the mushroom-soaking liquid—more if needed. Cover and cook, stirring occasionally, for 3 or 4 minutes. Add buttered noodles, toss it all together and serve.

CHILI CON CORNY

This chili dish is closely related to Chili Corn Pie. It is far simpler, less ostentatious. And it's definitely the one to fix if you feel like having chili, but are pressed for time.

PREPARATION TIME 7 MINUTES   **SERVES 4 TO 6**
COOKING TIME 10 MINUTES

- 1   green pepper, seeded and chopped
- 1   medium onion, chopped
- 1   clove garlic, minced
- 2   tablespoons oil

Sauté the 3 ingredients in oil for 5 minutes in a large skillet.

- 1   pound corn, frozen or canned
- 2   cups tomato purée
- 1   teaspoon chili powder
- ½   teaspoon salt
- 1   teaspoon soy sauce
       Few turns of pepper grinder

Add these ingredients to the sautéed vegetables and bring to a simmer.

- 2   tablespoons toasted wheat germ

Sprinkle over skillet mixture and stir.

- 1   cup grated cheddar cheese

When serving, garnish each portion generously with cheese. A simple, but ample, green salad goes well with this.

CHILI CORN PIE

This mildly spicy pie is a welcome and warming meal on a cold evening. There is a definite flavor of Mexico in the crunchy crust and heartily satisfying filling. Combined with a crisp salad and a glass of red wine, it has become one of our favorite suppers.

PREPARATION TIME 12 MINUTES*　　　　　　　　　　　　**SERVES 6**
BAKING TIME 25 MINUTES

Preheat oven to 350°.

1¾　cups cornmeal
3　tablespoons peanut oil
¾　cup hot vegetable stock or water (approximately)
½　teaspoon salt

Mix cornmeal, oil, liquid, and salt together with a fork until it forms a doughy paste. Press into an oiled 8- or 9-inch pie pan to form a crust. Set aside.

1　onion, chopped
½　cup chopped celery
½　cup chopped green pepper
2　tablespoons oil

Sauté onion, celery, and green pepper briefly in oil.

½　cup cooked corn, drained
2　cups cooked kidney beans, drained
4　tablespoons bean liquid
1　6-ounce can tomato sauce
⅓　cup chopped raw or roasted peanuts
½　teaspoon oregano
2　teaspoons chili powder (or more)
½　teaspoon ground cumin
¼　cup sliced pitted ripe olives
½　cup grated Jack or cheddar cheese

*Preparation time may be shortened by using a food processor to chop vegetables and nuts.

Combine sautéed vegetables with remaining ingredients *except* olives and cheese. Spread ⅓ of the cheese on surface of piecrust. Pour in filling and distribute evenly. Bake about 20 minutes. Remove from oven, spread sliced olives over the top and cover with remaining cheese. Return to oven for 5 minutes. Allow to cool slightly before cutting into wedges to serve.

MEDIEVAL LENTILS

Remember the "mess of pottage," in the Book of Genesis, that cost Esau his birthright? Well, here it is! We can't think why they ever gave it such an unappetizing name, for the dish is aromatic, savory, and delicious enough to drive any hungry person wild.

PREPARATION TIME 5 MINUTES   SERVES 6 TO 8
COOKING TIME 45 MINUTES

- 2 **tablespoons butter**
- 2 **tablespoons olive oil**
- 2 **cups sliced onions**

In a large, heavy-bottomed skillet, heat oil and butter until butter melts. Add onion slices and cook slowly about 20 minutes, stirring occasionally. Increase heat to moderate toward the end of cooking period to brown the slices a little.

- 1 **cup lentils, picked over and rinsed**
- 5 **cups water**

While the onions are cooking, place lentils and water in a large saucepan. Bring to boiling point, cover and reduce heat. Simmer about 20 minutes. Drain lentils and return to saucepan.

- 3 **cups vegetable stock**
- ½ **cup long grain rice**
- ¾ **teaspoon salt**
- 1 **teaspoon ground sumac***
- ¼ **teaspoon black pepper**

Add above ingredients to lentils. Reserve ⅓ cup of the onions and stir the rest into lentil mixture. Bring to a boil, reduce heat, cover and simmer about 25 minutes or until rice is tender. Spread the reserved onions over the top and serve.

Note: If you have cooked lentils, rice, and slow-cooked onions on hand, this dish will take only a few minutes. Just combine the cooked ingredients, add the seasonings, and moisten with a little vegetable stock. Place in a greased baking dish and bake in a 350° oven until heated through.

Menu Suggestion: Baked potatoes and a simple tossed green salad complete this hearty meal. Dessert should be light.

*Sumac is a Middle-Eastern spice. If not available, substitute ground cumin.

WALNUT-LENTIL PATTIES

Nearly everyone likes lentils. We still haven't heard of a dessert made with them, but they can be used in many other ways: in soup, as a hot vegetable, combined with other ingredients to make a main dish, or as a salad. These patties can be made from scratch, or with leftover cooked lentils.

PREPARATION TIME 20 MINUTES   SERVES 6
COOKING TIME 10 MINUTES

 2½ cups cooked lentils, drained

Purée the lentils in a food processor, or blender, or mash them well with a potato masher.

 2 cups walnuts
 2 cups fresh bread crumbs

Spread the walnuts and bread crumbs on separate shallow pans and toast lightly in a 400° oven, about 10 minutes.

 2 eggs, lightly beaten
 1 medium onion, finely chopped
 2 tablespoons tomato catsup
 ¼ teaspoon ground cloves
    Salt and pepper to taste
    Sour cream (if needed)

Chop the walnuts fairly fine in a food processor, blender, or nut grinder. Blend walnuts and bread crumbs with above ingredients, adding a small amount of sour cream if mixture seems too dry. Shape into patties.

 4 tablespoons butter or oil

Sauté patties in butter or oil over moderately low heat until nicely browned—about 5 minutes per side.

Menu Suggestion: Good accompaniments for Walnut-Lentil Patties would be Lemon Parsnips, spinach and raw mushroom salad, crusty rolls, and Fruit Mélange with Curaçao.

DIFFERENT SCALLOPED POTATOES

Enhancing the quality of scalloped potatoes with mushrooms and sunflower seeds isn't usual. But you'll agree, we're sure, that the enhancing was worth it.

PREPARATION TIME 10 MINUTES   **SERVES 4**
COOKING AND BAKING TIME 20 MINUTES

3   medium-sized potatoes

Peel and slice potatoes in ½-inch slices. Pressure cook the slices on rack over ½ cup water for 3 minutes. Set cooked potatoes aside.

¼   pound mushrooms, sliced
2   tablespoons butter

Sauté the mushrooms in butter for 5 minutes.

2   tablespoons whole wheat flour
1   cup milk

Add flour and milk to the mushrooms, stir and bring to a simmer.

3   hard-cooked eggs

Slice eggs and set aside.

1   cup grated cheddar cheese
1   tablespoon soy sauce
¼   cup sunflower seeds
   Pepper to taste

Add these ingredients to the simmering mixture. In a casserole, make layers of the potatoes, cheese-mushroom mixture, and egg slices. Repeat, using up the ingredients. The cheese-mushroom mixture should be the top layer. Bake for 15 minutes at 350°.

GOLDEN POTATO BAKE

The lowly potato comes into its own! Much credit really must go to its sauce which, incidentally, can be used on other vegetables instead of the customary hollandaise or cheese sauce—and with fine results.

PREPARATION TIME 15 MINUTES   SERVES 4 TO 6
COOKING TIME 8 MINUTES

- 5   medium potatoes, peeled and halved
- 1   large carrot, cut lengthwise

Pressure cook on rack over ½ cup water for 5 minutes. Set aside carrot and ½ cup of the cooked potatoes for sauce.

- 2   tablespoons butter
- 3   hard-cooked eggs
- 1   small onion, chopped
- 1   cup frozen peas
- ½   teaspoon salt
  Carrot-Potato Sauce (recipe follows)

Mash remaining potatoes with butter and eggs. Mix in other ingredients. Apportion this potato mixture into 4 to 6 ovenproof dishes and place under broiler. Remove when browned. Serve with generous amounts of sauce.

CARROT-POTATO SAUCE

- ¾   cup water
- 1   tablespoon oil
- 1   tablespoon lemon juice or half lemon and half vinegar
- ½   teaspoon salt
  Reserved carrot and potato

Put in blender and blend until smooth. Pour into a saucepan and heat.

CURRIED SOYBEANS

Although there are numerous ingredients in this entrée—especially if one counts the condiments accompanying it—it can be produced quickly. The spices are a matter of individual taste. You can even settle for just curry powder, in which case use twice the amount specified.

PREPARATION TIME 10 MINUTES   SERVES 4
COOKING TIME 10 MINUTES

- ½ teaspoon turmeric
- 1½ teaspoons ground cumin
- 1½ teaspoons curry powder
- ½ teaspoon cinnamon

Mix the spices together.

- 2 tablespoons butter

Melt the butter in a large skillet. Stir in the spices and cook for a minute or so.

- ½ cup chopped celery
- 1 medium onion, chopped
- 2 carrots, thinly sliced
- ¼ pound mushrooms, sliced
- 1 tablespoon cornstarch
- 1 cup dry soybeans, cooked
- ¾ cup water or soybean cooking liquid
- 4 ounces water chestnuts (optional)

Stir vegetables and other ingredients into the cooking spices. Simmer, covered, for 5 to 10 minutes, until vegetables are tender. Serve with condiments: salted peanuts, sliced green peppers, scallions, raisins, hard-cooked eggs—or any others that strike your fancy.

SOYBEAN PATTIES

"Patties" may very well be a euphemism for "burgers." This recipe, however, doesn't attempt to imitate, emulate, or substitute for the ubiquitous hamburger. Soybean patties are soybean patties.

PREPARATION TIME 10 MINUTES MAKES 8 TO 10 PATTIES
BAKING AND BROILING TIME 16 MINUTES

- 1½ cups cooked soybeans
- ⅔ cup sunflower seeds
- 3 tablespoons butter
- ¼ cup spaghetti sauce
- 1 small onion, chopped

Blend all ingredients to a paste consistency in blender or food processor. Put in mixing bowl. Preheat oven to 350°.

- ½ cup cooked soybeans
- ½ teaspoon chili powder
- 1 tablespoon soy sauce
- 1 stalk celery, chopped
- 1 tablespoon wheat germ

Add these to the bowl, mix all thoroughly and shape into patties. (If patties aren't firm, add more wheat germ.) Put patties on a buttered cookie sheet and bake 10 minutes. Then broil for a few minutes until brown.

Sliced cheddar cheese

Turn patties. Place a slice of cheese on the unbroiled sides. Broil until cheese melts.

SOYBEANS, ITALIAN STYLE

Any dish is less formidable if it can be prepared, in toto, on the range rather than in the oven. This one gives you a choice: skillet or casserole. Either way, this blend of pasta and beans makes for satisfying eating.

PREPARATION TIME 7 MINUTES

SERVES 4

COOKING TIME 10 MINUTES

> 1 cup macaroni

Cook according to package directions.

> 1 medium onion, chopped
> 1 stalk celery, chopped
> 1 tablespoon minced parsley
> ¼ cup oil

Sauté vegetables for five minutes.

> 1 cup chopped cabbage
> Salt and pepper to taste

Stir cabbage and seasonings into sautéed vegetables. Cook for a few minutes.

> 2 cups cooked soybeans
> 1 cup canned tomatoes

Add cooked macaroni, soybeans, and tomatoes to the cooking vegetables. Bring to a simmer.

> ½ cup grated Parmesan cheese or more
> Paprika

Remove skillet from heat, stir in cheese and sprinkle with paprika. Serve.

Variation: Spoon macaroni and vegetables from skillet into a casserole. Top with cheese and sprinkle with paprika. Set under broiler until cheese melts and browns.

SOYBEAN AND MUSHROOM STEW

Stew may sound plebian, but this stew has patrician qualities. It's very easy to prepare, and for the hungry, very satisfying. After all, it offers two good sources of protein: soybeans and cheese.

PREPARATION TIME 7 MINUTES   SERVES 4
COOKING TIME 30 MINUTES

- 3 cups cooked soybeans
- 1 6-ounce can tomato paste
- 1 medium onion, chopped
- 1 to 2 cloves garlic, crushed
- 1 cup sliced mushrooms
- 1 zucchini, about 6 inches long, thinly sliced
- 1 stalk celery, chopped
  - Salt to taste
  - Pinch of cinnamon, allspice, cloves, nutmeg
- ¼ to ½ cup grated cheddar cheese

Mix all ingredients in a 2-quart saucepan and simmer in water in which soybeans have been cooked, until vegetables are cooked. Add more water if needed. Transfer the stew to a serving dish, sprinkle with cheese, and serve.

ALMOND SPINACH ROULADE

When you're looking for a dish that's special—beautiful, different, and delicious—here's your answer. This roulade is especially good for entertaining, because it can be prepared in advance and refrigerated, needing only a short crisping in melted butter just before serving.

PREPARATION TIME 15 MINUTES   SERVES 6
BAKING AND CRISPING TIME 30 MINUTES

1	10-ounce package frozen spinach
2	tablespoons butter

Remove spinach from package, allow to thaw and drain well. Place butter in a 10-x-15-inch jelly roll pan and set in 375° oven for 5 minutes, or until butter is melted. Coat entire bottom of pan with melted butter.

2	cups milk
2	eggs
1	cup flour
1	teaspoon baking powder
½	teaspoon salt

Blend these ingredients in a food processor, blender, or electric mixer. Pour this batter into pan, spreading evenly over the bottom. Bake at 375° for 20 to 25 minutes or until it just barely starts to brown.

2	tablespoons butter
¾	cup chopped, slivered, or sliced almonds
½	teaspoon thyme
⅛	teaspoon nutmeg

While the oven pancake bakes, melt butter in a large, heavy skillet. Add almonds and sauté until lightly toasted, stirring frequently. Add thawed, drained spinach, thyme, and nutmeg, and stir to mix.

When pancake is baked, loosen it gently around the edges with a spatula and invert it, with a long edge facing you, on a clean dish towel. Spoon spinach mixture evenly over the top, spreading to all edges.

2   cups grated mild cheddar or Jack cheese

Sprinkle cheese over spinach, and using the towel as an aid, starting with the long edge roll up like a jelly roll. (If you wish to serve the roulade later, wrap in foil and refrigerate.)

3   tablespoons butter

Melt butter in large skillet. Cut roll in 6 portions. Sauté portions slowly, over moderately low heat, until browned and crisp on outside and heated through.

> **Sour cream**
> **Dijon mustard**

Serve with sour cream to which you have added mustard to taste.

EGGPLANT CHEESE STRUDEL

Once you've tried using strudel leaves or phyllo, you'll see that they have wonderful possibilities and you'll want to experiment with your own fillings. Here's a luscious, easy-to-make (but very impressive-looking) creation using eggplant. Don't be dismayed with the wrinkled, rather weird-looking pastry leaves as you butter them. A few rips and holes won't matter either, for it will all be beautiful in the end. See page 37 for information on handling phyllo.

PREPARATION TIME 30 MINUTES **4 SERVINGS**
BAKING TIME 35 MINUTES

   1   **medium eggplant, peeled and cubed**

Place eggplant in steamer over boiling water and steam about 5 minutes or until tender.

   2   **tablespoons butter**
   1   **medium onion, chopped**
   1   **large clove garlic, crushed**

While eggplant steams, melt butter in a large, heavy skillet and cook the onion, covered, over moderately low heat for 5 minutes. Remove the cover, add the garlic and cook a few minutes longer. When eggplant is done, drain it well and add it to the skillet, mashing it with the back of a spoon and mixing with the onion and garlic. Transfer this mixture to a bowl.

   6   **tablespoons butter (you may not need it all, but it's better to have too much than not enough)**

In the same skillet used for cooking the onion, melt butter. Pour it into a small bowl and place near area where you will work with the strudel.

   1½ **cups shredded Swiss or Jack cheese**
   2   **eggs, lightly beaten**
   ¼ **cup chopped parsley**
   ½ **teaspoon basil**
   ½ **teaspoon salt**
   ½ **cup dry bread-crumbs**

Add these ingredients to the eggplant mixture and stir well to blend. Taste for seasoning.

½ pound phyllo

Spread a lightly dampened cloth or towel on the counter. Butter an 8-x-8-x-2-inch square baking dish. Open the package of phyllo and remove approximately half of the leaves. Return the rest to the package, seal and refrigerate or freeze. Place the leaves in a stack on the damp towel. One at a time, brush the leaves with melted butter (it's not necessary to cover the whole leaf with butter—just a few broad swipes on each one). As you butter each leaf, place it in the baking dish, arranging the leaves on top of each other, fanning them around in a circular fashion so the edges hang down over the sides of the pan. When you have used half of the leaves, pour in the filling and smooth it on top. Fold the edges of the phyllo leaves over the filling. (It will look messy—never mind.) Continue buttering the remaining leaves, stacking them on top of the filling, folding in the edges to fit the size of the pan. Try to make the last few as neat as possible and tuck their edges down into the sides of the dish. Brush the top liberally with butter. With a sharp knife, cut the top layers of phyllo, down to the filling, into 4-inch squares (or 3-inch squares, if you prefer).

Bake at 375° until golden brown on top and puffy, about 35 minutes. (If strudel is made in advance to be reheated and served later, bake only 25 minutes.) Remove squares from pan to serving plates with a spatula. Pass sour cream for topping.

Note: Phyllo leaves come in varying sizes. Very large ones may have to be cut to a more convenient size and shape.

Menu Suggestion: Eggplant strudel is very easy to make, but it does take more time than some of our other dishes. Therefore we would suggest keeping the rest of the menu simple—a tossed salad, crusty French rolls, cookies and fruit for dessert.

EGGPLANT PARMIGIANA EXPRESS

The usual procedure of sautéing eggplant in oil, after dipping it in egg and bread-crumbs, is time-consuming and messy. Because each slice absorbs quite a lot of oil, this method is also caloric. Here's another approach with a delicious result.

PREPARATION TIME 10 MINUTES   SERVES 4 TO 6
BAKING TIME 30 MINUTES

Preheat oven to 425°.

> 1   medium-sized eggplant

Wash and trim eggplant; cut in ½-inch slices.

> ¼   cup mayonnaise
> 1   cup cracker or bread crumbs
> ⅓   cup grated Parmesan or cheddar cheese

Spread mayonnaise thinly on each side of eggplant slices and dredge in combined crumbs and cheese. Arrange slices on ungreased baking sheet. Bake at 425° about 15 minutes or until browned and fork-tender.

> ½   pound mozzarella cheese, sliced
> 1   cup Tomato Sauce (recipe follows)
> ½   cup grated Parmesan cheese

Layer the eggplant in a greased casserole, top each slice with mozzarella cheese and sprinkle with Parmesan. Spread some of the tomato sauce on each slice and pour the remainder over all. Sprinkle with the remaining Parmesan. Bake at 375° about 15 minutes.

TOMATO SAUCE

A quick tomato sauce can be made by diluting two 6-ounce cans of tomato paste with wine or water to make a thick sauce. Add ½ teaspoon basil, ½ teaspoon oregano, 1 crushed garlic clove, 2 teaspoons brown sugar, and salt and pepper to taste. If you have more than you need for this recipe, store remainder in refrigerator for later use.

SUMMER GARDEN CURRY BAKE

This is a good vegetable dish to make during the summer when zucchini and tomatoes are flooding the market. The spices add an unusual, pleasant zing.

PREPARATION TIME 12 MINUTES   SERVES 6
BAKING TIME 20 MINUTES

- 3   medium zucchini
- 3   tomatoes

Remove stem and blossom ends and slice the zucchini into ¼-inch slices. Place in steamer basket over boiling water and cook, covered, for about 5 minutes, or until barely crisp-tender. Slice tomatoes about ½ inch thick.

- ½   cup mayonnaise
- 2   teaspoons A.1. Sauce
- 1   tablespoon Dijon mustard
- 1   teaspoon curry powder
- 1   teaspoon fresh grated ginger root or ½ teaspoon ground ginger
- ½   cup toasted wheat germ
- ¼   cup grated Parmesan cheese
- 2   cups grated cheddar or Jack cheese

Combine the mayonnaise, A.1. Sauce, mustard, and other spices. In a greased, shallow baking dish, layer half the zucchini, tomatoes, mayonnaise mixture, wheat germ, and cheeses. Repeat layers, in the same order, with the second half of the ingredients, ending with the cheeses. Cover with foil and bake in a 350° oven for 20 minutes, or until cheese has melted and is bubbling.

SPINACH GRATIN

Spinach is much more popular now than it was back in Popeye's heyday. Its dark green leaves turn up in all sorts of guises— quiches, soufflés, salads, casseroles, and even in desserts. In the south of France, there's a famous pie made of apples, spinach, cheese, and nuts (Spinach Dessert Niçoise). Spinach Gratin is an especially good casserole to make when you have cooked brown rice on hand.

PREPARATION TIME 5 MINUTES   SERVES 4
BAKING TIME 20 MINUTES

Preheat oven to 325°.

2	pounds fresh spinach, cooked and drained or 2 10-ounce packages frozen chopped spinach, thawed, or cooked and well drained
1	cup cooked brown rice
1	cup grated cheddar cheese
2	tablespoons chopped parsley
½	teaspoon salt
⅛	teaspoon pepper
3	tablespoons catsup
1	tablespoon prepared horseradish
1	tablespoon melted butter

Combine all ingredients and pour into an oiled casserole.

3	tablespoons wheat germ
1	tablespoon melted butter

Combine wheat germ and butter and sprinkle over the top of the casserole. Bake at 325° for 20 minutes.

2	hard-cooked eggs, sliced
	Tomato sauce, warmed

Serve garnished with egg slices and pass tomato sauce for topping.

FROM A TO ZUCCHINI

This gathering of vegetables is rich in color, flavor, and texture. Though designed for easy top-of-range cooking, this main course ends up in a casserole just for appearance sake. Our children especially like the chewy topping. Undoubtedly, yours will too.

PREPARATION TIME 10 MINUTES   **SERVES 4**
COOKING TIME 15 MINUTES

- 1   onion, chopped
- 1   green pepper, seeded and chopped
- 1   clove garlic, minced
- ½ to 1 teaspoon oregano
- 2   tablespoons butter

Sauté the vegetables and oregano in butter for 5 minutes.

- 2   cups frozen mixed vegetables
- 4   cups thinly sliced zucchini

Add these to the sautéed vegetables, cover and cook over medium heat for 10 minutes.

- 1   medium tomato, diced
- 1   cup grated cheddar cheese
- ¼   cup toasted wheat germ
- ¼   cup chopped almonds
-     Mung bean sprouts

Stir in the diced tomato, one half the cheese, one half the wheat germ, and almonds. Spoon into a casserole. Mix the remaining cheese and wheat germ together and sprinkle on top the casserole. Put under broiler for a minute or two, browning lightly. Serve on a bed of mung bean sprouts.

BAKED EGGPLANT AND ZUCCHINI

The colors in this easy casserole are especially beautiful, because of the special way the vegetables and cheese slices are arranged in slanting, overlapping rows, so you can see them all. You don't hide a layer of one with a layer of another and then obscure the whole thing with a topping of crumbs. Instead, the deep brown-black of the unpeeled eggplant slices, soft pale green of the zucchini, melting golden cheese, and russet tomato sauce create a striking striated effect.

PREPARATION TIME 25 MINUTES   SERVES 6
BAKING TIME 20 MINUTES

- 1   medium eggplant
- 4   tablespoons olive oil
- 3   zucchini, 6 to 8 inches long
      Salt and pepper

Wash eggplant well; do not peel. Slice off ends and cut into ½-inch slices. Cut each slice in half crosswise. Pour 2 tablespoons of the oil into a shallow, rimmed baking pan and brush it evenly over the bottom. Lay the eggplant slices on the pan and brush each one with the remaining oil, using more if necessary. Cover the pan tightly with aluminum foil and place in a 400° oven. Bake until tender, but not mushy, about 12 to 15 minutes.

While the eggplant bakes, wash zucchini, remove stem and blossom ends and cut into ½-inch slices. Arrange slices in steamer basket and steam over 1 inch of boiling water until crisp-tender, about 5 to 7 minutes. Drain.

- 1   1-pound can Italian plum tomatoes
- ½   cup minced onion
- 2   tablespoons olive oil
- 2   tablespoons tomato paste
- 1   bay leaf, crumbled
- 1   teaspoon basil
- ¼   teaspoon each, thyme and oregano
- 1   clove garlic, crushed
       Salt and pepper to taste

Drain tomatoes, setting aside the liquid, and purée them in a blender or food processor. Put onions and oil in a small, heavy saucepan. Stir to mix, cover, and steam over moderately low heat about 6 minutes. Add tomato purée, and remaining ingredients and simmer, uncovered, about 10 minutes. Sauce should be of spreading consistency. If it is not, add a little more tomato paste.

¼   **pound Jarlsberg cheese, thinly sliced**
    Reserved tomato liquid

In a greased, shallow baking dish, arrange the eggplant and zucchini in slanting, overlapping alternating rows, spreading each row with tomato sauce and topping each with slices of cheese. Pour in enough of the tomato liquid to cover the bottom of the dish. Cover tightly with aluminum foil and bake at 400° for 15 minutes. Uncover and bake 5 minutes longer.

ZUCCHINI STUFFED WITH MUSHROOMS AND ALMONDS

We often choose this dish when invited to a potluck dinner party and asked to "bring something for the vegetarians." It's easy to do, but apparently looks as if it required some effort. Everyone seems to enjoy it—vegetarians and non—so we always make plenty.

These stuffed zucchini can be prepared up to the point of final baking and refrigerated as much as a day ahead. Once they're baked, it's best not to reheat them as the zucchini shells may become soft and limp, making them difficult to serve. If you are taking them with you, try to arrange to bake them after your arrival.

PREPARATION TIME 25 MINUTES   **SERVES 8**
BAKING TIME 20 TO 25 MINUTES

    4   large zucchini, 7 to 8 inches long

Wash zucchini, trim off the ends and cut in half lengthwise. Steam over 1 inch of boiling salted water, 4 minutes. Remove squash from steamer with tongs and plunge immediately into a large pan of cold water. Drain, cut side down, on paper towels. With a grapefruit spoon, scoop out a trough in each squash half to hold the filling. Chop the scooped out flesh, squeeze it dry between paper towels and set aside.

    2   tablespoons butter
    2   green onions (scallions), minced
    1   cup finely chopped fresh mushrooms, squeezed dry between paper towels
    1   clove garlic, crushed
         Chopped zucchini flesh

Melt butter in a heavy-bottomed skillet over low heat and sauté the onions, covered, about 5 minutes. Uncover, raise heat to moderately high and add the garlic, chopped zucchini flesh, and mushrooms. Sauté 2 or 3 minutes longer. Remove from heat.

    ⅓   cup grated Swiss cheese
    ½   cup almonds (ground in blender or food processor)
    ½   cup dry bread crumbs or more
    ¼   teaspoon ground cloves
         Salt and pepper

Stir all ingredients into filling mixture.

1	egg
½	cup sour cream

Beat egg and sour cream together with a wire whisk and blend into the filling mixture. Mixture should be thick enough to mound up when spooned into the zucchini shells. If it isn't, add more crumbs.

¼	cup bread crumbs
¼	cup grated Swiss cheese
	Melted butter

Arrange zucchini shells in a well-buttered shallow baking dish large enough to hold them in one layer. Heap the stuffing into each half. Mix bread crumbs and cheese and sprinkle over tops. Drizzle with melted butter. Bake at 400° for 20 to 25 minutes.

NEW ENGLAND PRESSURE-COOKED DINNER

How can one explain that this simple dish is such an ongoing favorite in our family? Well, the flavors of the four vegetables do blend in a taste-appealing way. And, as wine tasters might say of a wine, the vegetable combination *is* straightforward and without pretense.

PREPARATION TIME 10 MINUTES   SERVES 4 TO 6
COOKING TIME 5 MINUTES

- 4   medium potatoes, peeled and cut in ½-inch slices
- 4   medium onions, quartered
- 4   medium carrots, split lengthwise
- 1½ pounds cabbage, cored and cut in chunks
- 1   teaspoon caraway seeds

Put in pressure cooker and cook for 5 minutes, until vegetables are tender. (Follow pressure cooker instruction book for amount of water and how much food can be cooked at one time.)

Butter
Cheese, grated or shredded (cheddar, Swiss, Muenster)
Salt and pepper to taste

Add butter, cheese, and seasonings to individual servings.

VEGETABLE, FRUIT, AND NUT CASSEROLE

To combine vegetables, fruits, and nuts is especially newsworthy, because the result is delicious. A colorful, nutritious, "conversation piece" main course.

PREPARATION TIME 7 MINUTES   **SERVES 4 TO 5**
BAKING TIME 30 MINUTES

Preheat oven to 375°.

- 2   medium apples, peeled, cored, and cut in chunks
- 1   20-ounce bag of frozen mixed vegetables (any variety)
- 3   tablespoons toasted wheat germ
- ½   cup coarsely chopped walnuts
- ¼   cup sunflower seeds
- ½   cup apple juice
- 1   tablespoon butter

Butter a 1½-quart casserole. In it, combine apples, vegetables, and wheat germ. Sprinkle walnuts and sunflower seeds over mixture. Pour apple juice over all. Dot with butter and bake.

COTTAGE CHEESE AND NOODLES

There are hundreds of cheese and noodle recipes around, but this one happens to be an old favorite. It's substantial and nourishing, with just a bit of extra zip to it. And it's *so easy!*

PREPARATION TIME 10 MINUTES   SERVES 4 TO 6
BAKING TIME 20 MINUTES

> 3   cups broad egg noodles

Cook noodles in boiling salted water for 10 minutes. Drain.

> 1   cup small curd cottage cheese
> 1   cup sour cream
> 2   tablespoons minced onion
> ½   teaspoon salt
> 1   clove garlic, minced
> 1   teaspoon A.1. Sauce
> ¼   teaspoon Tabasco
> ¼   cup fine dry bread-crumbs

Combine drained noodles with above ingredients.

> ¼   cup grated Parmesan or cheddar cheese

Place noodle mixture in buttered 1½- or 2-quart casserole and sprinkle with cheese. Bake at 350° for 20 minutes, or until heated through.

12-MINUTE SPAGHETTI

Undoubtedly, spaghetti purists would scoff at a spaghetti that can be prepared—sauce and all—in a mere 12 minutes. Just a taste could win them over. And they might even be intrigued by the idea that the water in which the spaghetti was cooked was then used in making the sauce.

PREPARATION TIME 5 MINUTES   SERVES 3 TO 4
COOKING TIME 12 MINUTES

    2   cups water
    1   teaspoon salt

Put water and salt in a 2-quart saucepan and bring to a boil.

    ¼   pound thin spaghetti (spaghettini)

Break spaghetti in half and drop into boiling water. Maintain a slow boil for 8 minutes. One to 1½ cups of water should remain at the end of the 8 minutes.

    1   1-pound can tomatoes
    1   6-ounce can tomato paste
    1   medium onion, quartered
    1   clove garlic, peeled
    1   teaspoon oregano
    1   tablespoon red wine
    1   tablespoon oil
    1   teaspoon brown sugar
         Sprinkling of dillweed or fresh dill
         Salt and pepper
         Grated Parmesan cheese

Put above ingredients except cheese in blender. Blend at lowest speed for 5 seconds. Mix with spaghetti and cooking water and simmer for 4 minutes. Serve with grated cheese.

PASTA PROVENCAL

This recipe may look forbidding, because it has such a long list of ingredients, but it's actually very simple to execute. All you have to do is lightly cook fresh (or frozen) vegetables, combine them with a glistening garlic-and-basil-scented sauce of cream and cheese, and toss it all with spaghetti. It's beautiful to look at and makes a hearty meal. Serve with crusty French bread and a chilled white wine. A fruit dessert goes well with this.

PREPARATION TIME 10 MINUTES   SERVES 4
COOKING TIME 15 MINUTES

- 1 cup broccoli flowerets
- 1 cup asparagus cut in 1-inch diagonal slices
- 1 cup sliced zucchini
- 1 cup cauliflower flowerets
  Boiling water
  Salt

Arrange vegetables in a large steamer in separate groups, and steam over boiling salted water until barely tender, but still crisp, about 4 minutes. Drain and chill vegetables under cold running water. Drain again and set aside. (This may be done in advance.)

- ¾ pound thin spaghetti

Cook spaghetti in a large pot of boiling salted water until *al dente*, about 10 minutes.

- 1 tablespoon butter
- ½ cup sliced almonds

While spaghetti cooks, melt butter in a heavy pot large enough to hold all the vegetables and spaghetti. Sauté the nuts until they are crisp and lightly browned. Remove them with a slotted spoon and set aside to drain on paper towel.

- ¼ pound fresh white mushroom caps
  Olive oil

If mushrooms are large, halve or quarter them, otherwise leave them whole. Add oil to the pot as needed and sauté the mushrooms quickly over high heat until lightly browned. Remove them with a slotted spoon and set aside.

10 cherry tomatoes, halved
1   clove garlic, crushed
   Salt and pepper

In the same pot sauté the tomatoes with the garlic over moderately low heat, adding a little oil if needed. Season to taste with salt and pepper. Remove tomatoes with a slotted spoon and add to the mushroom caps.

¼ cup butter
1   clove garlic, crushed
⅓ cup grated Parmesan cheese
¾ cup heavy cream or more
1½ teaspoons chopped fresh basil or ½ teaspoon dried basil

Still using the same pot, melt the butter and add garlic, basil, cheese, and cream, stirring to blend. Add the cooked, drained spaghetti and toss to coat with sauce. Add the vegetables and mushrooms and toss gently over moderate heat until all is piping hot. If sauce is too thick, thin with a little more cream. Sprinkle in the toasted nuts and toss again. Taste for seasoning. Serve on warm plates with extra grated Parmesan on the side.

Variations: Endless combinations of vegetables are possible—just choose those that cook in the same length of time, or cut them so they will all be done at once.

LAZY DAY PIZZA

Some traditional pizzas take hours to produce. They are indeed delicious, but we doubt if we'd feel like making them very often. So it's good to know that an excellent pizza can emerge from the oven in much less than an hour, and that you can whip one up whenever you get the urge. If you enjoy pizza as much as we do—that will be often. *Mangiamo!*

PREPARATION TIME 15 MINUTES   MAKES ONE 14-INCH PIZZA
RISING TIME 10 MINUTES
BAKING TIME 15 TO 20 MINUTES

> **2 cups whole wheat flour**

Pour flour into a large mixing bowl.

> **1 package (1 tablespoon) active dry yeast**
> **¾ teaspoon salt**

Add yeast and salt to flour and stir to blend.

> **1 cup hot tap water**
> **1 tablespoon cooking oil**
> **1 teaspoon honey**

Add these ingredients to flour mixture and beat vigorously until well mixed. Cover with plastic wrap and place in a warm spot for 10 minutes. Punch down and place dough in a greased 14-inch pizza pan. Press with fingers to evenly cover bottom of pan and up the sides to form a rim. Preheat oven to 425°.

> **2 cups tomato sauce**
> **1 cup sliced mushrooms, sautéed**
> **½ cup sliced onions, sautéed**
> **½ cup sliced, pitted ripe olives**
> **½ teaspoon crumbled oregano**
> **½ teaspoon crumbled basil**
> **6 ounces mozzarella cheese, shredded or sliced**
> **¼ cup freshly grated Parmesan cheese**
> **Olive oil**

Spread sauce on dough, distribute remaining ingredients evenly over the top, ending with a sprinkling of olive oil. Bake at 425° for 15 to 20 minutes until crust is golden brown and cheese is melted.

Variation: Here's another topping that's extra crispy and features flavorful almonds:

1	teaspoon oil
1	cup shredded mozzarella cheese
2	medium tomatoes, thinly sliced
¾	cup sliced mushrooms
2	tablespoons sliced green onions
1	teaspoon mixed basil and oregano
¼	teaspoon thyme
¼	cup slivered almonds
1	tablespoon freshly grated Parmesan cheese

Brush oil on prepared pizza dough and sprinkle mozzarella cheese evenly over the surface. Top with remaining ingredients in given order, ending with the Parmesan. Bake on the lowest rack of a 400° oven until crust is browned and cheese is melted and bubbling. Remove from oven.

1	tablespoon chopped parsley

Sprinkle top of pie with parsley and cut in wedges to serve.

MOSTLY MUSHROOMS PIZZA

There are two unusual things about this pizza. First, there is no long-cooking tomato sauce in the topping. Second, the pizza dough needs only 15 minutes of rising time instead of the usual 1 to 1½ hours. If you have a heavy-duty mixer, such as KitchenAid, equipped with a dough hook, the preparation time will be reduced because you can be slicing and chopping mushrooms, grating cheese, and making a salad while the dough hook kneads for you. But even if you do the whole process manually, it should take well under 45 minutes from start to finish.

PREPARATION TIME 20 MINUTES　　　　　　**MAKES TWO 13-INCH PIZZAS**
RISING TIME 15 MINUTES
BAKING TIME 20 MINUTES

Preheat oven to 400°.

12 dried black mushrooms
Hot water

Rinse the mushrooms and cover with hot tap water. Set aside while you make the dough.

1 cup lukewarm water
1 package (1 tablespoon) active dry yeast
1 teaspoon sugar

In a large mixing bowl, sprinkle yeast over the water and allow to stand a minute or two. Stir in sugar until dissolved and let stand about 5 minutes.

1 teaspoon salt
1 tablespoon soft butter or margarine

Add salt and shortening and beat well until smooth.

3 cups all-purpose flour (approximately)

Stir in 1½ cups of flour gradually and beat well. Add enough of the remaining flour to make a soft dough, one that is just barely manageable. Knead until smooth, 5 or 6 minutes. Divide dough into two pieces and shape each piece into a ball. Flatten each ball slightly and then, holding it in your hands, pull and stretch it gently while rotating it until it is about 6 or 7 inches in diameter. Lay the circle of dough on a lightly floured board and roll to approximate size of the pizza pan. Place on the lightly oiled pan and stretch to fit, building up a rim around the edge. Cover loosely with plastic wrap and set aside to rise 15 minutes.

1 **pound fresh mushrooms, sliced**
1 **teaspoon oregano**
1 **teaspoon basil**
  Salt to taste
  Freshly ground black pepper to taste
2 **cups shredded mozzarella cheese**
  Olive oil

Scatter a layer of sliced fresh mushrooms over the dough in each pan. Drain the dried mushrooms (saving liquid for future use), and chop or shred them. Scatter these over the fresh ones. Sprinkle oregano, basil, salt, and pepper over each pizza, dividing the amounts given between the two pans. Scatter the mozzarella over all and sprinkle generously with olive oil. Place pans on two shelves in the oven. After 10 minutes, switch position of the pans. Bake 10 minutes more, or until dough is crisp and lightly browned around the edges and the cheese is bubbling.

PESTO WITH PASTA

Pesto sauce, served over steaming hot pasta, is one of the joys of summer. We usually plant a long row of basil next to the tomatoes. There are two good reasons for this: First, like love and marriage, basil and tomatoes go together; so we often pick them at the same time. Second, whiteflies, which attack tomatoes, *hate* the smell of basil; so the basil becomes a natural bug repellent! You could hardly ask for a more convenient combination. Pesto is not totally confined to summertime, because the base can be frozen and brought out in January for a taste of July.

PREPARATION TIME 5 MINUTES   SERVES 6
COOKING TIME 10 MINUTES

- **2 to 3** cups fresh basil leaves, washed and dried
- **½** cup fresh parsley leaves, washed and dried
- **2** tablespoons pine nuts
- **1** teaspoon salt, or to taste
- **½** teaspoon freshly ground black pepper
- **⅓** cup best-quality olive oil

Put herbs and nuts in blender or food processor bowl. Sprinkle in salt and pepper. Start motor, slowly pour in oil and process until a paste is formed. (At this point, if you are not planning to use the pesto base immediately, freeze it flat in a tight plastic bag. When ready to use, allow it to thaw overnight in the refrigerator.)

- **1** pound thin spaghetti
- **6** quarts boiling water

Just before serving time (and no sooner), drop the spaghetti into the hot boiling water and cook for 10 minutes. While the pasta cooks, warm a large shallow serving bowl and 6 dinner plates and prepare the sauce:

- **½** cup freshly grated Parmesan cheese
- **2** cloves garlic, minced
- **3** tablespoons ricotta cheese

By hand, mix the above ingredients into the pesto base.

2 to 3 tablespoons spaghetti cooking water

Call your family or guests to the table so there will be no time for the pasta to cool off. Stir 2 tablespoons of the hot cooking water into the pesto sauce. Drain the pasta, pour it into the warmed serving bowl and pour the pesto sauce over it. Toss well and serve on the warm plates.

Note: If fresh basil is not available, you may substitute additional parsley. The Italian flat-leaved variety has the best flavor. Pine nuts are sometimes hard to find. We have substituted toasted sunflower seeds with good results. Pesto sauce is delicious on hot vegetables, baked potatoes, in soups, and as a dressing for salads—especially tomato salad.

NUTTY NOODLE CASSEROLE

This casserole comes under the heading of "Easy to Make, but Takes Time to Bake." It's really good!

PREPARATION TIME 15 MINUTES   SERVES 4
BAKING TIME 1 HOUR

Preheat oven to 350°.

1	cup chopped cashew nuts
1	cup chopped onions
1	cup chopped fresh mushrooms
1	cup chopped celery
1	cup fine egg noodles
1	cup crisp Chinese noodles
1	cup vegetable stock
2	tablespoons oil
½	teaspoon salt

Mix all ingredients together, place in an oiled casserole and bake at 350° for 1 hour. That's all there is to it!

MACARONI PIZZA

At one and the same time, this dish can conceivably satisfy two simultaneous cravings—a craving for macaroni and a craving for pizza.

PREPARATION TIME 5 MINUTES   SERVES 6
COOKING TIME 7 MINUTES
BAKING TIME 20 MINUTES

> 1   7-ounce package macaroni

Cook according to package directions. Drain.

> 2   eggs
>   Few turns of pepper grinder

Beat eggs, add pepper and macaroni. Pour into buttered 9-inch baking dish. Bake in preheated 400° oven for 10 minutes.

> 1   cup tomato sauce
> 1   teaspoon oregano
> 1½ cups shredded mozzarella or Swiss cheese

Mix sauce and oregano. Spread over baked macaroni. Top with cheese and return to oven for 10 more minutes. Cut into portions and serve.

MACARONI MIREPOIX

This is your old favorite, macaroni, with a little French twist. Mirepoix is a combination of finely diced carrots, onions, and celery, sautéed in butter. Add it to a simple cheese sauce, fling in a bit of oregano and *voila*—you have macaroni and cheese elegant!

All this is done on top of the stove, no need to use your oven. Great for campers, too.

PREPARATION TIME 6 MINUTES   **SERVES 6**
COOKING TIME 15 MINUTES

- 1   7- or 8-ounce package elbow macaroni

Cook macaroni according to package directions. Drain.

- ¼   cup butter
- ¼   cup each shredded carrots, chopped celery, and chopped green onions
- ¼   cup flour
- ½   teaspoon salt
- 1   teaspoon oregano
- 2   teaspoons prepared mustard

While macaroni is cooking, melt butter in a large heavy-bottomed saucepan that will hold about 3 quarts. Drop in vegetables and cook, stirring, over moderate heat for 2 or 3 minutes. Add flour, salt, oregano, and mustard and stir well to blend. Cook, stirring over low heat 2 minutes. Remove pan from burner.

- 2   cups milk

Stir in milk gradually, return pan to burner and heat to boiling, stirring constantly. Boil and stir 1 minute. Remove from heat.

- 1½ cups shredded cheddar cheese
  - Tomatoes (optional)
  - Parsley (optional)

Add cheese to the pan and stir until melted, returning pan to low heat if necessary to melt the cheese. Do not boil. Stir in the macaroni and heat to serving temperature. Garnish with tomato slices and chopped parsley, if available.

KASHA-CHEESE SKILLET

You might say this is a skillet rather than a casserole, because it is made in a skillet and not in a casserole. The skillet does the whole job—sautéing, broiling, serving. This simplification, obviously, makes for ease of preparation. And the result tastes so good that you'd prepare this dish again and again even if it were difficult to make.

PREPARATION TIME 7 MINUTES   **SERVES 4 TO 6**
COOKING TIME 15 MINUTES

    1   large onion, chopped
    4   tablespoons butter

Sauté onion for 5 minutes in a large ovenproof skillet.

    1   cup medium kasha (roasted buckwheat kernels)
    1   teaspoon salt
    2   cups water

Stir kasha, salt, and water into sautéed onions and bring to a boil. Reduce heat to low. Cover and cook 5 minutes. Remove from heat.

    1   cup cottage cheese
    1   cup frozen corn

Mix cheese and corn with the kasha, tossing lightly.

    1   cup grated cheddar cheese
    2 to 3 tomatoes

Sprinkle contents of skillet with cheese. Slide skillet under broiler for 3 to 5 minutes until cheese melts. Serve with tomato slices or wedges.

BULGUR AND VEGETABLES

For the record, and your cooking, bulgur and cracked wheat are interchangeable. It should also be said that this recipe bears a resemblance to Confetti Rice which features rice and vegetables. They differ in one vital aspect—their flavor.

PREPARATION TIME 10 MINUTES   SERVES 6
COOKING TIME 20 MINUTES

    3   cups water
    1   cup bulgur (cracked wheat)
    1½   teaspoons salt

Bring water to a boil. Add bulgur and salt. Cover and cook over low heat for 20 minutes.

    ¼   cup oil
    1   medium onion, chopped
    1   green pepper, seeded and chopped
    2   stalks celery, chopped
    4   large tomatoes, chopped

Sauté vegetables in oil for 5 minutes. Combine vegetables and bulgur.

    1   tablespoon honey

Stir in honey and serve.

LENTIL-WHEAT-BROCCOLI PILAF

Pilaf is usually made with rice. This recipe, we're sure you'll agree, challenges rice's supremacy as a pilaf staple. Be sure to savor the wonderful contrast between hot pilaf and cold yogurt.

PREPARATION TIME 5 MINUTES   **SERVES 4**
COOKING TIME 35 MINUTES

- ½   cup lentils, rinsed
- 2   cups water
- 1   teaspoon salt

Put lentils, water, and salt in saucepan and bring to boil. Lower heat, cover and simmer for 20 minutes.

- 3   tablespoons oil
- 1   medium onion, chopped
- 1   stalk broccoli, sliced (½ cup to 1 cup sliced)
- ½   cup cracked wheat
      Yogurt

Sauté onions, broccoli, and cracked wheat in oil until vegetables are fairly soft. Pour lentils and water over the sautéed mixture, bring to boil, cover and simmer for 15 minutes more. Serve topped with yogurt.

SPANISH PILAF

A mélange of rice, vegetables, fruits, and nuts makes this pilaf a beautiful centerpiece for a summer buffet table. The vibrant colors are straight from the Costa del Sol, and the fragrance is redolent of oranges and spices. Like all good buffet dishes, it can be made ahead and reheated. Served with rolls, a salad, and chilled white wine, it makes a beautiful meal. Since this dish is on the light side, a sinfully rich dessert could be the grand finale. How about Chocolate Mousse? Or Cheesecake?

PREPARATION TIME 12 MINUTES   **SERVES 6**
COOKING TIME 15 MINUTES

- 3 tablespoons butter
- 2 medium onions, sliced
- 2 cloves garlic, minced
- 1 sweet green pepper, seeded and sliced
- 1 sweet red pepper, seeded and sliced

In a large, heavy-bottomed saucepan, melt the butter over medium heat. Add onions, garlic, and peppers and cook, stirring for 5 minutes, or until onions are tender.

- 2 large ripe tomatoes, chopped
- 1 seedless orange, peeled, sliced crosswise and diced
- 2 ripe bananas, peeled and sliced
- ⅓ cup sliced or shredded almonds
- 2 tablespoons sunflower seeds
- ¼ cup raisins
- 2 teaspoons turmeric
- ½ teaspoon salt

Add all ingredients to the pan and stir gently to combine. Cook, stirring occasionally, 3 or 4 minutes longer.

- 4½ to 5 cups cooked brown rice
- 1 mild sweet onion, thinly sliced and separated into rings
   Parsley or mint sprigs

Stir rice into the mixture and simmer, stirring occasionally, 5 minutes, or until heated through. Pile the pilaf into a warm shallow serving platter and garnish with onion rings and herb sprigs.

RICE AND NUT CASSEROLE

The beauty of preparing this dish is that it's simply a matter of mixing all its ingredients together. Do you have to sauté an onion? No. How about folding in egg whites? Absolutely not. Here are the ingredients and the very little that you do with them in order to produce this crunchy taste sensation.

PREPARATION TIME 7 MINUTES   SERVES 4 TO 6
BAKING TIME 35 MINUTES

2	cups cooked brown rice
1	cup grated cheddar cheese
1	cup grated Swiss cheese
½	teaspoon salt
2	cups milk
3	eggs
1	onion, chopped
3	tablespoons minced parsley
½	cup chopped almonds
½	cup chopped walnuts
¼	cup sunflower seeds

Mix all ingredients in a well-oiled ovenproof casserole. Bake for 35 minutes in a 350° oven, until set and nicely brown.

CONFETTI RICE

If you have cooked kidney beans, brown rice, and sautéed onions on hand, this colorful stove-top casserole will go together in a flash. Rice and beans, that classic combination in so many of the developing countries, is the perfect example of a complementary protein dish.

PREPARATION TIME 10 MINUTES
COOKING TIME 20 MINUTES

SERVES 6

- 1 tablespoon butter
- ½ cup chopped onion

In a large, heavy-bottomed saucepan with a lid, melt butter over moderately low heat and sauté onion, covered, for about 5 minutes, stirring occasionally.

- ¾ cup vegetable stock
- 3 teaspoons chili powder
- ½ teaspoon ground cumin
- ¼ teaspoon oregano
- 1 teaspoon salt

Stir the stock and seasonings into the onion and simmer 3 minutes.

- 3½ cups cooked brown rice
- ½ cup sliced pitted ripe olives
- ½ green pepper, seeded and chopped
- 3 tablespoons chopped pimineto
- 2 cups kidney beans, cooked and drained

Stir all ingredients into the onion-stock mixture, cover and simmer about 10 minutes or until well heated through, stirring occasionally.

Turn rice and bean mixture into an attractive, heated casserole.

- 1 ripe avocado, peeled, pitted, and sliced
   Lemon juice
- ⅓ cup chopped Spanish peanuts

Dip avocado slices in lemon juice and arrange decoratively on top of the casserole. Sprinkle with peanuts. Serve at once or keep warm in a very low oven.

RICE PATTIES

These herb-flavored patties are crunchy and satisfying. They are a protein dish and go well with a leafy vegetable or buttered carrots and a baked potato.

PREPARATION TIME 10 MINUTES   SERVES 4
COOKING TIME 15 MINUTES

    1½ cups cooked brown rice
    1   cup finely chopped or ground salted peanuts
    ⅔ cup finely chopped or ground sunflower seeds
    ½ cup chopped onion
    2   eggs, lightly beaten
    ½ teaspoon thyme
    ½ teaspoon sage
    ½ teaspoon salt (if needed)

Mix all ingredients together.

    2   tablespoons cooking oil

In a large, heavy-bottomed skillet heat the oil over moderate heat. Make patties of the rice mixture by packing it into a ½-cup measure, pressing it in firmly with the back of a spoon. Drop the patties into the oil and flatten each one with a spatula into a round about 3 inches in diameter. Lower heat to moderately low, and cook for 10 minutes on one side. Turn, cook 5 minutes on second side and serve.

CURRIED RICE AND PEAS

If for no other reason than this recipe, you should always have cooked brown rice in the refrigerator and frozen peas in the freezer. With those two ingredients on hand, curried rice and peas can be made quickly and easily. Thick slices of tomato, flavored with oil, and onion rings, make a delicious, just-right accompaniment.

PREPARATION TIME 5 MINUTES   SERVES 4
COOKING TIME 10 MINUTES

> 1 medium onion, chopped
> 3 tablespoons butter
> ¼ to ½ teaspoon curry powder

Sauté onion 5 minutes, stirring to combine with curry powder.

> 4 cups cooked brown rice
> 1½ cups frozen peas
>   Salt and pepper to taste
>   Wheat sprouts (optional)

Add these ingredients to the sautéed onion. Heat through and serve.

GARBANZOS PLUS RICE

You may not be aware that garbanzos constitute an important part of the diet of Southern Europe and India. Rice, of course, is also a staple for millions. It therefore seems fitting—though this is a dreadful non sequitur—that these two be combined in a delicious dish that only requires you to mix a few ingredients.

PREPARATION TIME 3 MINUTES   SERVES 4 TO 6
COOKING TIME SUFFICIENT TO HEAT

> 4   **cups cooked brown rice**
> 3   **cups cooked garbanzos**
> 3   **tablespoons butter**

Mix together and heat to serving temperature while stirring.

> ¼   **cup honey or more if desired**
>   **Sprinkling of wheat sprouts (optional)**

Add to combined rice and garbanzos and mix thoroughly. Serve with our favorite Salsa Piquante on your favorite salad.

GARBANZO-RICE PIE

We've named this pie in honor of its crust, for the crust is that good. All in all, a substantial entrée. Handsome looking, too. As well-rounded as a soufflé, and as promising as a sunrise—which its colors suggest.

PREPARATION TIME 10 MINUTES   SERVES 4 TO 6
BAKING TIME: CRUST 15 MINUTES, ENTIRE PIE 25 MINUTES

- 1½ cups cooked brown rice
- ½ cup garbanzo flour*
- 1 cup whole wheat flour
- ½ cup wheat germ
- 2 tablespoons oil
- ½ teaspoon salt

Preheat oven to 425°. Mix all ingredients together by hand or in food processor. Pat out into an 8- or 9-inch pie pan. If dough is sticky, add more flour. Prick bottom and sides of crust with fork and bake for 15 minutes.

- 1 onion, chopped
- 1 clove garlic, minced
- ½ pound cheddar cheese, grated
- 2 eggs
- ¼ cup catsup
- 1 tablespoon oil
- 1 teaspoon oregano

While crust is baking, mix these ingredients together. When crust is done, lower oven heat to 350°. Spoon ingredients into baked pie crust and bake until set, about 25 minutes.

* Available in gourmet shops.

MAMA'S MAMALIGA

Because Mother came from Rumania, we grew up on mamaliga. In fact, we used to think that the "mama" in mamaliga referred to Mother. This is a hearty, staple food of the Slavic farmers who ate what was plentiful and at hand—corn from the fields and cheese made from goat's milk. We've never outgrown our taste for mamaliga, but have made a few changes and additions of our own.

PREPARATION TIME 2 MINUTES   SERVES 4 TO 5
COOKING TIME 8 MINUTES

>   4   **cups cold water**
>   1½ **cups yellow cornmeal**
>   1   **teaspoon salt**

In a large, heavy saucepan bring to a boil 3 cups of the water. Mix the remaining cup of cold water in a bowl with the cornmeal, add salt and stir with a fork. Add to the boiling water.

>   2   **tablespoons butter**

Stir in the butter, bring to a boil, reduce the heat to low and cover. The mixture will be very thick. Cook 7 minutes, stirring once or twice. Remove lid, raise heat to medium. Run a large spoon several times around the edge of the cornmeal to loosen it from the sides. Lift pan from the burner from time to time, bouncing it up and down sharply, until you can feel the cornmeal loosen from the bottom. Invert the pan over a platter, and the mass will fall out like a cake.

>   **Creamed large curd cottage cheese**
>   **Canned pear halves, chilled**

Cut cornmeal into wedges and top with cottage cheese. Serve with pear halves on the side. A tray of crisp raw vegetables is a good accompaniment.

Variation: For a different taste (and a more authentic presentation) we sometimes split the cornmeal "cake" into two layers by pulling a heavy string crosswise through the center. We pour warm garlic butter over the bottom layer, sprinkle it with 1½ cups crumbled feta cheese, add the upper layer and top with sour cream. Cut in wedges. Serve with Antipasto Salad for a great meal!

HERB QUICHE

Purists may be aghast at the mere thought of a quiche without a crust. Such a speedily made quiche exists, however, and eventually we'll reveal its formula. But right now, we offer a quiche for herb fanciers—and with it, not only one easy, quick crust, but a choice between two. The crust is prepared first.

Quiche Crust

PREPARATION TIME 10 MINUTES   SERVES 6
BAKING TIME 10 MINUTES

Preheat oven to 425°

> 1½ cups flour
> 1   teaspoon sugar
> ½   teaspoon salt

Sift ingredients into a 9-inch pie pan.

> 7   tablespoons (scant ½ cup) salad oil
> 2   tablespoons milk

Mix oil with milk and pour over dry ingredients. Mix thoroughly, then press mixture into bottom and sides of pan. Bake at 425° for 10 minutes.

Crust variation: Use same procedure as above with the following ingredients:

> 1½ cups whole wheat flour
> ½   cup soy flour
> ½   teaspoon salt
> ¼   cup oil
> 1   tablespoon poppy seeds
>   Ice water (enough to make a firm dough)

Quiche Filling

PREPARATION TIME 10 MINUTES
BAKING TIME 20 MINUTES

⅓   **pound cheese, shredded (Swiss, Muenster, or Port du Salut)**
½   **teaspoon basil**
¼   **teaspoon crushed marjoram**

Combine cheese and herbs; sprinkle evenly in prebaked crust.

2   **eggs**
1   **cup cream**
½   **teaspoon salt**
    Pepper to taste

Beat these ingredients and pour over the cheese in crust. Bake 20 minutes at 400°.

ASPARAGUS SOUFFLETTES

The neat, timesaving trick here is dividing the batter into individual servings, which will cut the baking time to a fraction. But that's not all! These puffs are whipped up in the food processor or blender; the eggs don't have to be separated, and the batter can be mixed ahead of time and held at room temperature for several hours, or refrigerated for an even longer period. To top it all off, the finished soufflettes don't deflate as quickly as their classic counterparts when removed from the oven.

Since you're likely to have the ingredients on hand, all you need to do is memorize the formula in order to always be the cool host when guests pop in unexpectedly, and you'd like to ask them to stay for lunch or brunch.

PREPARATION TIME 10 MINUTES   SERVES 6
BAKING TIME 15 TO 20 MINUTES

Preheat oven to 375°.

> 2   **cups lightly cooked asparagus, drained**

Cut into pieces, reserving 6 of the nicest tips to use as a garnish.

> **Soft butter**

Butter generously six 1-cup ramekins or individual soufflé dishes.

> 6   **eggs**
> 6   **tablespoons milk plus 2 tablespoons melted butter or ½ cup heavy cream**
> ¼   **cup grated Swiss or Jarlsberg cheese**
> 1   **teaspoon prepared mustard**
> ¼   **teaspoon salt**
> ⅛   **teaspoon freshly grated nutmeg**

Place ingredients in 6 to 8 cup blender or in food processor and blend until smooth. With motor running, add asparagus and blend a moment or two.

> 1⅓ **cups (about 11 ounces) ricotta or cream cheese**

With motor running, add ricotta in large spoonfuls (or cream cheese in pieces). After all cheese has been added, continue blending 4 or 5 seconds longer. Pour batter into ramekins, dividing the amount equally and filling them about ¾ full. Place them on the middle shelf of the oven and bake at 375°, 15 to 20 minutes or until puffed and set. Unmold onto individual serving plates. Top with Quick Hollandaise Sauce (recipe follows), and garnish with the reserved asparagus tips.

Variations: As you probably realize, this recipe is a good one for leftovers. You can use nearly any vegetable, except very watery types such as zucchini and spinach. Vary your seasonings according to the flavor of the main ingredient—for example, with broccoli you might substitute ¼ teaspoon cayenne pepper for the nutmeg. Herbs may be added, and other grated cheeses used. Sautéed chopped onions or mushrooms can be used as the main flavoring ingredient. Ripe avocado is delicious. If cooked vegetables aren't available, substitute ½ pound of grated cheese in addition to the ¼ cup already in the recipe. When using cheese, reduce the salt to a pinch.

Instead of making individual soufflettes, the mixture may be baked in a well-buttered 5-cup ring mold, increasing the baking time to 35 to 40 minutes. After unmolding onto serving platter, the center may be filled with another vegetable—tiny, new boiled potatoes, for example.

QUICK HOLLANDAISE SAUCE

You need a blender or food processor for this.

¼ pound (1 stick) butter

Heat butter until very hot, but not browned.

3 egg yolks
1 tablespoon lemon juice
Dash cayenne pepper
⅛ teaspoon salt

Put these ingredients in blender. Cover, turn on motor and remove center section of cover. Slowly pour in hot butter. Sauce will thicken as you pour.

BROCCOLI FRITTATA

This has been referred to as an Italian version of an omelet. No matter what its national origin, busy, discriminating people will find that it has quite a few virtues. Only two pans are needed. And, except for a few minutes under the broiler, the cooking is done on the range. In addition, we found it a new taste sensation.

PREPARATION TIME 7 MINUTES   SERVES 4
COOKING TIME 20 MINUTES

    1   **10-ounce package frozen chopped broccoli**

Cook according to package directions.

    3   **tablespoons butter**
    4   **ounces fresh mushrooms, sliced**
    1   **medium onion, chopped**

In a large ovenproof skillet, sauté mushrooms and onions for 5 minutes until tender, but not brown.

    6   **eggs**
    ½   **teaspoon salt**
    Pepper to taste

Beat eggs, add seasoning, and stir in cooked broccoli. Pour this mixture over mushrooms and onions. Cook over medium heat until the eggs set, about 7 minutes.

    ⅓   **cup grated Parmesan cheese**

Sprinkle the eggs and broccoli with cheese. Broil about 6 inches from heat for 2 to 3 minutes, until nicely browned. Cut in wedges to serve.

212 | Main Dishes

MUSHROOM SPECTACULAR

Have your family and/or guests already seated at the table when you serve this savory golden puff. It is very simple to put together, and the result is, indeed, spectacular. If it must wait a moment or two while you round everyone up, leave it in the turned-off oven with the door ajar until ready for the grand presentation.

PREPARATION TIME 10 MINUTES*   SERVES 4 TO 5
BAKING TIME 20 TO 25 MINUTES

Preheat oven to 450°.

3	tablespoons butter or margarine
1	small onion, chopped
1	green pepper, seeded and chopped
½	pound fresh mushrooms, sliced

Melt 2 tablespoons of the butter in a heavy, 2- to 3-quart frying pan, with oven-proof handle, on top of the stove. Sauté onion and green pepper briefly and remove from pan with slotted spoon. Add remaining tablespoon of butter to skillet and sauté mushrooms on medium high heat, pouring off liquid as it accumulates, until lightly browned and fairly dry. Remove from pan, add to onions and green pepper. (Save the mushroom liquid to add to your vegetable stock pot.)

¼	cup (½ stick) butter or margarine
3	eggs
¾	cup milk
¾	cup flour
½	teaspoon salt
2	green chiles, seeded and chopped (optional)
⅓	cup grated mild cheddar cheese
1	cup tomato sauce or taco sauce

Put butter in the skillet and place in preheated oven. While the butter is melting, beat the eggs in an electric mixer until light. Gradu-

*Preparation time may be further reduced by using a food processor to chop the vegetables. A food processor or a blender can cut the mixing of batter ingredients to 1 minute.

ally add the milk while beating, then slowly add flour and salt. Mix well. Stir in the sautéed mushrooms, onion, green peppers, and if desired, the green chiles. Remove pan from the oven and pour the batter into the melted butter. Return to oven and bake until puffed and golden brown. Sprinkle top with grated cheese and cut into wedges to serve. Pass a warm, spicy tomato or taco sauce for topping.

Variations: Substitutions can be as varied as the leftovers you may have in your refrigerator. Cooked vegetables such as peas or corn, sliced ripe olives, chopped chives, chopped scallions, etc. Just keep the amounts of your additions equivalent to those in the recipe above.

GUACAMOLE SOUFFLÉS

For a special luncheon or brunch, these chartreuse puffs are spectacular, visually and otherwise. Soufflés have an undeserved reputation for being tricky to create, when actually they're nothing more than a simple white sauce combined with eggs.

We recommend using only perfectly ripe California avocados for this dish, because of their rich, nutty flavor. Otherwise, you just might blow it—or, as the French say, *souffler*.

PREPARATION TIME 15 MINUTES   SERVES 4
BAKING TIME 20 MINUTES

Preheat oven to 350°.

> 3   tablespoons butter
> 3   tablespoons flour
> 1   cup milk

Put ingredients in blender or food processor and blend until well mixed, about 30 seconds. Pour mixture into a small saucepan and bring to a boil, stirring constantly with wire whisk. Allow to boil 1 minute, stirring. Remove from heat and set pan in cold water to cool mixture to room temperature. Change the water several times to speed cooling.

> 1   ripe avocado, peeled, pitted, and diced
> 2   teaspoons lime or lemon juice
> 1   clove garlic, minced
> ½   small onion, peeled and quartered
> 8   drops Tabasco sauce
> 1   canned green chile, rinsed and seeded (optional)

While sauce is cooling, place ingredients above in blender or food processor and process until smooth. Scoop mixture into a bowl, and combine with the cooled white sauce.

> 3   eggs, separated
> ½   teaspoon salt
> ¼   teaspoon cream of tartar

With a wire whisk, beat the egg yolks into the avocado mixture one at a time. Beat in salt. Whisk until light in color and frothy. In large bowl of electric mixer, beat egg whites until foamy, add cream of tartar and beat until whites are very stiff, shiny, and form sharp peaks when beater is lifted. Add about ¼ of the whites to the avocado mixture and blend in with a wire whisk. With a rubber spatula, gently fold the avocado mixture into the remaining egg whites. Do not overblend. Pour soufflé into greased individual 1½ cup ramekins or soufflé dishes, and bake at 350° for 15 to 20 minutes, or until puffed and set.

Menu Suggestion: Guacamole Soufflés need only a tossed salad, or perhaps Antipasto Salad, and rolls to accompany them. Dessert should definitely be eggless, for example, Fruit Mélange with Curaçao.

CHILES RELLENOS PUFF

Mexican *chiles rellenos con queso* (cheese-stuffed chile peppers, dipped in a soufflé-type batter and fried in oil), are a favorite delicacy. Here's a version that eliminates the oil and much of the toil, because the whole dish bakes at once like a puffy oven omelet.

PREPARATION TIME 15 MINUTES   SERVES 4 TO 6
BAKING TIME 30 MINUTES

> 2   7-ounce cans whole green chiles
> ½   pound Jack cheese

Remove seeds and pith from chiles by splitting along one side and rinsing under cool water. Spread chiles on paper towels to dry. Cut cheese into pieces about ½ inch wide, ½ inch thick, and a little shorter than the chiles. Tuck a piece of cheese inside each chile, and fold chile over to enclose the cheese. Arrange chiles side by side on the bottom of a well-buttered baking dish (about 2 quart size).

> 5   eggs
> ⅔   cup milk
> 6   tablespoons flour
> ¾   teaspoon baking powder

Beat the eggs until foamy. Add milk, flour, and baking powder and beat until fairly smooth. Pour egg mixture over the chiles, making sure that the surfaces of all chiles are moist.

> 1   cup shredded cheddar cheese
> ¼   cup sunflower seeds

Sprinkle cheese and seeds over the top of the batter and bake, uncovered, in a 375° oven for about 30 minutes, or until set when gently shaken.

> ¼   cup sliced, pitted ripe olives
> 2   cups warmed, spiced Tomato Sauce (see page 172)

Garnish the casserole with olives and pass the tomato sauce as a topping.

Top-of-the-stove variation: You can make chiles rellenos on the griddle, too, as small individual souffléed puffs. Prepare and stuff the chiles as above. Separate 4 eggs. Beat the whites until they hold rounded peaks. Beat the yolks with ¼ cup flour, 1 tablespoon water, and ¼ teaspoon salt. Fold yolks gently into whites with rubber spatula, using an over and under motion. Don't try to eliminate all white streaks from the batter; about 12 folds should do it.

On a large griddle, melt 2 tablespoons of butter over moderate heat. Drop mounded tablespoons of the batter onto the heated griddle (as many as it will accommodate). Place a stuffed chile in the center of each mound and spoon batter over the top of each chile to enclose it. Cook over moderately low heat for 3 or 4 minutes, then turn and cook several minutes longer. Repeat with remaining chiles and batter, adding butter to the griddle as necessary. Serve with taco sauce.

QUICHE SANS CRUST

By not having a crust, this quiche is easier to make and ready for the table sooner. It's obvious that the recipe is concerned only with essentials—not a pastry shell, but the shell's substance. Note, too, that it's all made in a big iron skillet from which it's served.

PREPARATION TIME 20 MINUTES   SERVES 4 TO 6
BAKING TIME 25 MINUTES

- ¼ cup salad oil
- 1 medium onion, chopped
- 1 clove garlic, minced
- 2 medium tomatoes, diced
- 1 small (¾ pound) eggplant, peeled and diced
- 2 cups sliced zucchini
- 6 mushrooms, sliced

Heat oil in large iron skillet. As each ingredient is prepared, put it in the skillet and stir with the others. Preheat oven to 400°.

- 4 eggs
- ½ cup grated Parmesan cheese
- ½ pound cheddar cheese, grated
  Salt and pepper to taste

Beat eggs. By this time the sautéing vegetables should be fairly tender; remove from heat and mix eggs with them. To this mixture stir in half of each of the cheeses and salt and pepper. Top with remaining cheese, slide skillet into the 400° oven for 25 minutes. Cut into wedges to serve.

RICOTTA CHEESE PANCAKES

These light, tender, high-protein pancakes are perfect for breakfast, lunch, or dinner. Serve them with cold applesauce, sprinkled with cinnamon.

PREPARATION TIME 3 MINUTES   SERVES 3
BAKING TIME 10 MINUTES

- 3   eggs
- 1   cup ricotta cheese
- 2   tablespoons vegetable oil
- 2   tablespoons wheat germ
- 2   tablespoons flour
- ¼   teaspoon salt

In a blender or food processor, combine ingredients and blend until smooth, scraping sides of container as necessary. Pour batter onto a heated, lightly greased griddle in 3- or 4-inch rounds. Bake over moderate heat until bubbles form on the surface. Turn and bake on the other side.

Variation: Cottage cheese may be substituted for the ricotta. If you would like to serve these pancakes as a protein-rich dessert, add 2 teaspoons sugar to the batter. Dust the hot pancakes with a little powdered sugar and serve with sliced fruit or berries.

Note: Ricotta pancakes can be made ahead and reheated. After baking, cool them on racks. When ready to serve, place them on a shallow pan in a single layer. Cover with foil and heat at 375° for 5 minutes.

ZUCCHINI PANCAKES

Zucchini is one of the ever-present vegetables. It's available all year round in the markets, and during the summer months the home gardener sometimes finds himself knee-deep in a "zucchini problem." What to do with all this squash? Make zucchini pancakes.

PREPARATION TIME 15 MINUTES   **SERVES 4**
FRYING TIME 4 TO 7 MINUTES

> 2   medium zucchini, grated
> ¼   cup chopped onion
> ½   teaspoon salt

Toss zucchini and onion with salt and allow to stand 10 minutes.

> 2   eggs, lightly beaten
> ½   teaspoon salt
> 1   tablespoon chopped fresh basil or 1 teaspoon dried basil
>   Freshly ground black pepper to taste

In a large bowl, blend ingredients together. Drain zucchini and onions and press out excess liquid. (This is easily done with a potato ricer.) Stir vegetables into the eggs.

> **Fine bread or cracker crumbs (as needed)**

Stir in crumbs until mixture holds together.

> 1   tablespoon butter
>   Oil (as needed)

In a large, heavy skillet melt butter and add enough oil to cover bottom of pan to ⅛ inch. When oil is hot, drop in batter in large spoonfuls (an ice-cream scoop works beautifully), and flatten each cake slightly. Fry until pancakes are crisp and brown on each side.

> **Sour cream**

Serve pancakes with cold sour cream.

Menu Suggestion: Zucchini Pancakes are excellent with Broiled Tomatoes Parmesan and buttered corn, on or off the cob.

Vegetable Side Dishes

There are those who argue that vegetables require only butter, salt, and pepper, and that this is the quickest and easiest way to prepare them. Playing devil's advocate, we'll answer that it would be even quicker and easier to eat them without this seasoning. However, if you are going to add butter, salt, and pepper, you're obviously trying to improve the vegetable's taste. So why not anise on carrots, curry on new potatoes, dill on cauliflower? As a change from butter, salt, and pepper, why not?

We hope you enjoy the Aniseed Carrots, the Curried New Potatoes, the Dilled Cauliflower—and all the others.

GREEN BEANS ITALIANO

This recipe produces a crisp, multiflavored green bean. It's certainly giant steps removed from the standard green bean side dish, cooked until tasteless and presumably salvaged by the addition of butter, salt, and pepper.

PREPARATION TIME 10 MINUTES   SERVES 4 TO 6
COOKING TIME 7 TO 10 MINUTES

   1   **pound green beans**

Cut off ends and wash. Cut beans on a diagonal with kitchen shears, making 2 to 3 pieces per bean.

  ¼   **cup water**
  2   **tablespoons butter**
  1   **clove garlic, crushed**
  ½   **teaspoon oregano**

Cook green beans in a covered pan with these ingredients.

  ½   **cup sliced almonds**

Stir in nuts when beans are crisp-tender and nearly all the water has evaporated. Cook for about a minute.

  3   **tablespoons sour cream**

When ready to serve, remove pan from heat and fold sour cream into the bean mixture.

ANISEED CARROTS LOPEZ

Anise is a sweet-smelling herb related to the carrot family. Maybe this kinship accounts for the fact that carrots and the seeds of the anise plant go together so beautifully. Glazed carrots prepared this way always look as if they were meant to be photographed in living color for a gourmet food magazine.

PREPARATION TIME 4 TO 6 MINUTES   SERVES 4
COOKING TIME 12 TO 15 MINUTES

    1½ pounds small carrots

Peel carrots and leave them whole. (If you must use large carrots, halve or quarter them to approximate the size of small carrots.) Pressure-cook the carrots until tender, usually about 4 minutes. Drain and dry.

    ¼   pound butter
    1   tablespoon brown sugar
    ½   teaspoon whole aniseed
    1   teaspoon salt
    ½   teaspoon freshly ground black pepper

In a large, heavy-bottomed skillet, melt the butter over moderate heat. When the foam starts to subside, stir in the sugar, aniseed, salt, and pepper. Add the carrots and roll them around in the mixture to coat well. Cook slowly, over low heat, stirring or shaking the pan to turn the carrots occasionally, until they are glazed and have turned a deep, rich color.

SESAME CAULIFLOWER

By itself, cauliflower looks rather pale and uninteresting. Toasted sesame seeds, green onion, and sweet pepper liven up its appearance and add piquancy to its flavor.

PREPARATION TIME 3 MINUTES   SERVES 6
COOKING TIME 12 MINUTES

    1   head cauliflower
    1   teaspoon lemon juice

Separate cauliflower into flowerets and steam over 1 inch of boiling water to which you have added the lemon juice. Cook until barely tender when pierced, about 10 minutes.

    ¼   cup (½ stick) butter
    3   tablespoons chopped onion

While cauliflower steams, melt butter in a large, heavy frying pan and sauté the onion until soft. Add steamed cauliflower and stir gently to combine with onion.

    4   tablespoons toasted sesame seeds
    ⅓   cup chopped green onions
    ⅓   cup chopped sweet red or green pepper
         Salt and pepper

Stir in these ingredients and cook for 1 minute, stirring, to heat through and blend flavors.

PERUVIAN LIMAS

Lima beans originated in South America and are named for the capital of Peru. We've no idea what herbs pre-Columbian cooks might have used to accentuate the rich, distinctive flavor of their beans, but here's a combination we like. With the addition of Duxelles or sautéed mushrooms, this dish rises to gourmet pinnacles.

PREPARATION TIME 7 MINUTES   SERVES 4
COOKING TIME 15 MINUTES

   3 to 4 pounds fresh lima beans in shell or 2 packages frozen

Shell beans and steam in steamer basket over 1 inch of boiling water until tender, about 10 minutes. Drain.

   ¼   **cup (½ stick) butter, melted**
   1   **tablespoon chopped shallots or chives or scallions**

In a large, heavy saucepan, sauté shallots until soft.

   1   **teaspoon lemon juice**
   1   **tablespoon chopped parsley**
   1   **tablespoon fresh tarragon leaves or 1 teaspoon dried
       Salt and pepper to taste**

Add these ingredients to shallots and stir in beans.

   ¼   **cup sautéed sliced mushrooms or 1 tablespoon Duxelles
       (optional)**

Add mushrooms to beans, cover and simmer until heated through.

KASHA-PEA DELIGHT

Peas are peas, as alike as peas in a pod, but the combination of kasha and peas is something altogether different. What's more, it can be made in just a few minutes.

PREPARATION TIME 5 MINUTES   SERVES 4 TO 6
COOKING TIME 5 MINUTES

   3   **cups water**
   ½   **teaspoon salt**

Put salted water on high heat.

> 1   medium-sized onion, chopped
> 2   tablespoons butter

While the water is coming to a boil, sauté the onion for 5 minutes

> 1   cup medium kasha (roasted buckwheat kernels)
> 1   cup frozen peas
>   Soy sauce

Pour kasha into boiling water, lower heat and cook covered for 5 minutes. A minute before kasha is done, stir in the frozen peas and sautéed onions. Add soy sauce to taste.

BROILED TOMATOES PARMESAN

Tomatoes are very good when simply sprinkled with some chopped herbs, salt, pepper, and a little oil and broiled for about 5 minutes. For a change, though, you might like to try them with this puffy golden topping. Even wan winter tomatoes can be exciting.

PREPARATION TIME 5 MINUTES   **SERVES 6**
BROILING TIME 5 MINUTES

> 6   firm, ripe tomatoes
> 1   tablespoon oil
>   Salt and pepper

Core tomatoes and slice them in half horizontally. Oil a shallow pan or dish large enough to hold the tomatoes in one layer. Arrange the slices on it, cut side up. Sprinkle with salt and pepper.

> ½   cup mayonnaise
> ½   cup grated Parmesan cheese
> 4   green onions, finely chopped

Mix ingredients together with a fork. Spread a generous amount of mayonnaise mixture on each tomato half. Place under broiler and broil until puffed, bubbly, and golden. Serve immediately.

REAL REGAL SPINACH

The little boy in the cartoon who said, "I say it's spinach and to hell with it," obviously must have had a traumatic spinach experience. Spinach can have the life cooked out of it. Spinach can be served plain—utterly plain. Having said all this, we give you the blueprint for a little-boy-proof spinach.

PREPARATION TIME 5 MINUTES   SERVES 6
COOKING TIME 8 MINUTES

> 4   tablespoons butter
> 2   medium onions, chopped
> 2   cloves garlic, crushed

In a large skillet, sauté the onions and garlic for 5 minutes.

> 2½ to 3 pounds spinach, washed, dried, and torn into small pieces

Add spinach and sauté 3 minutes. Remove from heat.

> ⅓   cup grated Parmesan cheese
> ⅓   cup toasted wheat germ
> ½   cup sour cream

Blend these ingredients with the sautéed vegetables. Heat at low temperature.

BUTTER PECAN SQUASH CASSEROLE

This savory casserole is worthy of a place on your Thanksgiving feast table. Acorn squash is good, but we use butternut squash when we can find it, because its flesh is so firm, succulent, and beautifully colored—and the flavor is something like that of chestnuts. It's no problem to peel if you cut it into quarters, remove the seeds and stringy pulp, cut each quarter into several pieces and steam them, peel and all, over a small amount of boiling water for 15 minutes, or until fork tender. The skin will pull off easily then. Please use real butter for this dish.

PREPARATION TIME 20 MINUTES   SERVES 8 TO 10
BAKING TIME 15 MINUTES

4   pounds butternut squash (about 4 cups cooked)

Cook and peel squash as described above. Place pieces in a large mixing bowl and mash, but don't try to make the texture supersmooth.

¼   cup (½ stick) butter
2   tablespoons finely chopped green onion
1   teaspoon crushed dried rosemary
½   teaspoon salt
¼   cup coarsely chopped pecans

Beat in the butter, onion, rosemary, and salt. Turn the mixture into a 1½-quart casserole and sprinkle with the chopped pecans. Bake in a 400° oven 15 to 20 minutes or until thoroughly heated.

Note: You may prepare this casserole ahead of time and refrigerate it, covered. When ready to use, bake in a 400° oven 25 to 30 minutes or until heated through.

LEMON PARSNIPS

Parsnips have a rather sweet, yet slightly pungent taste that blends well with lemon. When they're steamed in butter until just tender, with crisp, brown edges here and there, and laced with lemon juice, they become a vegetable to cherish. See what you think.

PREPARATION TIME 5 MINUTES   SERVES 4
COOKING TIME 9 MINUTES

> 1   **pound parsnips**
> 4   **tablespoons butter**
> 6   **tablespoons vegetable stock**

Cut off ends of parsnips and peel with a swivel peeler. Cut into ¼-inch crosswise slices. In a medium-sized skillet with a lid, melt butter over moderately high heat. Add parsnips and toss to coat with butter. Pour in stock. Cover, bring to a boil and steam about 7 minutes, stirring once or twice, or shaking pan to keep parsnips from sticking.

> 2   **tablespoons lemon juice**
>   **Salt and pepper**

Just before serving, stir in lemon juice, season with salt and pepper and toss over high heat for a few minutes until piping hot.

CURRIED NEW POTATOES

These golden, crusty potatoes, with a little nip of curry and mustard, are especially good with Walnut-Lentil Patties or Soybean Patties.

PREPARATION TIME 5 MINUTES   SERVES 4 TO 6
COOKING TIME 30 MINUTES

> **2** pounds small new potatoes, washed, quartered, and dried
> **½** cup (1 stick) butter

Melt butter in a large heavy pot, such as a Dutch oven. Add potatoes and cook over moderate heat, uncovered, for 10 minutes, stirring occasionally.

> **1** teaspoon curry powder
> **1** teaspoon dry mustard

Sprinkle spices over the potatoes and stir well to mix. Reduce heat to low, cover, and cook 10 to 15 minutes or until potatoes are tender.

> **¼** cup chopped scallions
> Salt and pepper

Uncover, stir in chopped scallions and seasoning. Increase heat to medium high and cook, stirring and tossing, until some of the potatoes are crisp and browned.

Note: To use leftover boiled or baked potatoes, reduce the amount of butter to 5 tablespoons. Add cut up potatoes to the melted butter, and cook, stirring, about 5 minutes. Stir in spices and continue cooking until some potatoes are lightly browned and crisp. Add scallions and seasonings, heat through and serve.

ZUCCHINI WITH CHERRY TOMATOES

This dish will be at its very best if you can find small, young zucchini. For superior flavor and appearance, it should be made just before serving.

PREPARATION TIME 5 MINUTES   **SERVES 6 TO 8**
COOKING TIME 6 MINUTES

      1½ pounds zucchini

Cut zucchini into ½-inch slices. Steam them over 1 inch of boiling water until barely tender, about 5 minutes. Drain well.

     3   **tablespoons butter**
     2   **cups cherry tomatoes, halved**
     1   **teaspoon salt**
     1   **teaspoon dried basil**
         Freshly ground pepper

Melt butter in a large, heavy skillet. Add zucchini and remaining ingredients, toss gently and taste for seasoning. Simmer about 1 minute, or until the tomatoes are heated.

     1   **tablespoon toasted sesame seeds**
     2   **tablespoons chopped parsley**

Add seeds and parsley, toss, and serve.

OVERNIGHT SUCCESS PICKLES

Some members of our family have always had a furtive fondness for pickles. We considered this more of a vice than a virtue, because we were pretty sure that although pickles might not be really *bad* for us, there probably wasn't much about them that was good, either. Therefore, we were pleasantly surprised to learn that our most eminent modern dieticians consider pickles to be a beneficial food—an aid to digestion and a sharpener of appetites! We hope that knowing this won't spoil anyone's fun.

These easy pickles require no cooking or processing and are kept in the refrigerator. Fresh-tasting, crisp, and sweetened with honey, they will keep for several weeks, but we doubt that they will be around that long. Choose cucumbers that are firm, fresh, and long in proportion to their circumference.

PREPARATION TIME 12 MINUTES
PLUS STANDING TIME   MAKES ABOUT 1 QUART

- 3 large cucumbers, about 1½ inches in diameter or 7 or 8 small cucumbers
- 1 medium onion, chopped
- 1 sweet red or green pepper, stemmed, seeded, and chopped
- 1 tablespoon kosher salt or other noniodized salt
- 2 teaspoons celery seed

If cucumbers have been waxed, peel them. Otherwise, scrub them well and slice thinly. In a large bowl, stir together cucumbers, onion, pepper, salt, and celery seed until well combined. Let stand 1 hour.

- ½ cup honey
- ½ cup distilled white vinegar

Thoroughly mix honey and vinegar. Pour over pickles and stir to blend. Place in a covered glass container and refrigerate. Pickles are ready to eat in 24 hours.

Desserts

Obviously, desserts are meant to be enjoyed—and they are. At the same time, people worry about sugar which isn't supposed to be healthful, and there's also fretting about gaining weight. Enjoyment, in other words, isn't quite as complete as it might be.

Bearing all this in mind, we've picked recipes that aren't completely evil; they do, after all, contain wholesome ingredients. Some are substantial, too. These are perfect for rounding out a meal that may, for example, be weak in proteins. The frivolous recipes—and this may appear downright rationalization—do supply an occasional necessary indulgence. Abstinence, we feel, can very well be a path straight to an orgy. And since this is so, we don't believe in going overboard and outlawing the sweet and the beautiful completely. So there's Chocolate Mousse and Banana Ice Cream Pie. From this you might think that restraint left us completely, but it didn't. This is made evident, to give but one example, by our Cheeseless Cheese Cake.

To the charge that we're encouraging the consumption of desserts by making them easy to prepare, we plead guilty. But we do deserve some credit for sneaking in wheat germ here and sunflower seeds there and for insinuating soybeans into a pie!

BAKED APPLES ALLEGRO

Nothing for dessert? If you can round up some firm, crisp, tart-sweet apples, you can have one ready in 15 minutes. If you're not calorie-counting—or if dinner was light—add whipped cream or a scoop of ice cream.

PREPARATION TIME 5 MINUTES   SERVES 4
BAKING TIME 10 MINUTES

> 4 to 5 medium-sized apples
> 1 tablespoon melted butter
> Brown sugar (as needed. Adjust to tartness of apples.)
> 1 teaspoon brandy
> ¼ teaspoon cinnamon

Preheat oven to 400°.

Peel apples, cut them into quarters and remove the cores. Arrange them in a single layer, core side down, in a buttered baking dish. Brush apples with melted butter, sprinkle with sugar, brandy, and cinnamon. Bake in oven 10 minutes, or until apples are tender. Remove from oven, turn apples over in sauce that has collected in the bottom of the pan, and serve warm.

APRICOT YOGURT PIE

This has to be one of the easiest pies around! Barely a few minutes of your time (plus several hours of chilling in the refrigerator) produces an elegantly smooth, refreshing dessert.

PREPARATION TIME 5 MINUTES   MAKES ONE 9-INCH PIE
CHILLING TIME 3 HOURS OR LONGER

> **12**   ounces softened cream cheese
> **1**   cup plain yogurt
> **3**   tablespoons honey
> **1**   teaspoon vanilla extract

Beat all ingredients together until smooth.

> **1**   baked 9-inch Nifty Nut Crust or Graham Cracker Crus.
> **½**   cup drained chopped canned apricots

Pour half the cheese-yogurt mixture into the crust, spreading it over the bottom. Spoon apricots evenly over this filling and cover them with the rest of the mixture. Chill for at least 3 hours, or overnight. Thirty minutes in the freezer will speed setting time.

> **¾**   cup chopped nuts

Sprinkle nuts over top of pie before cutting into wedges to serve.

Variation: Other fruits may be used, fresh, frozen, or canned. Just be sure they're well drained before adding them to the pie.

BANANAS PRALINE

One of the simplest desserts—and one of the most surprisingly delicious—consists of frozen banana chunks. The bananas may be served after dinner as a confection for nibbling, with picks supplied for spearing them.

We like to cut the bananas Oriental style (1-inch diagonal slices), dip and roll the pieces in crushed praline, then freeze them in a single layer on a waxed paper-lined baking sheet until solid. After the chunks are frozen, they can be removed from the tray, dropped into plastic freezer bags, sealed and returned to the freezer until needed. Don't let them stand long after removing from the freezer for serving. If they thaw too much, they quickly lose their charm.

Here's a quick and easy way to make the praline for crushing.

PREPARATION TIME 5 MINUTES
PLUS FREEZING TIME

- ¼ cup cashew butter or peanut butter
- ¼ cup butter
- 1 cup brown sugar, firmly packed

In a small saucepan, combine the nut butter, regular butter, and sugar. Cook and stir over low heat, until sugar melts, about 3 minutes.

- 2 cups crisp rice cereal, coarsely crushed
- 1 cup salted cashews

Remove pan from heat and stir in rice cereal and nuts. Spread on a buttered shallow-rimmed pan and allow to cool, then break into pieces and store in airtight containers. To use for the above recipe, crush as much as you need in a blender or food processor.

Variations: The bananas can also be rolled in ground nuts or a combination of ground nuts and grated chocolate. Wheat germ is an excellent coating, too. These make a good after-school snack.

FRUIT MÉLANGE WITH CURACAO

As we have all surely learned from Thanksgivings past, overeating is an enemy of enjoyment. There are times when a light fruit dessert is the perfect finale to a memorable meal. This mélange is one we have relied on for many years to strike a gentle final chord.

PREPARATION TIME 5 MINUTES   **SERVES 6**
CHILLING TIME 1 HOUR OR MORE

- **6 cups mixed fresh fruit of your choice: strawberries, mangoes, bananas, peaches, nectarines, blueberries, etc.**
- **6 tablespoons frozen orange juice concentrate**
- **¼ cup orange Curaçao liqueur**

Peel and pit larger fruit, and slice into bite-sized pieces. Place the fruit in a large serving bowl (a glass one is particularly effective). Combine the undiluted orange juice concentrate with the orange liqueur and pour over the fruit. Chill fruit mixture thoroughly before serving.

DESSERT SPREAD FOR FRUIT AND COOKIES

A touch of brandy or fruit liqueur gives a distinctive lift to this light dessert. Its principal ingredient is ricotta, the creamy bland cheese commonly used in lasagne.

PREPARATION TIME 5 MINUTES   **SERVES 4 TO 6**

- **2 cups (1 pound) ricotta**
- **3 to 5 tablespoons confectioners' sugar**
- **2 tablespoons brandy**
- **¼ teaspoon cinnamon**

Place all ingredients in mixer and beat until smooth. Spoon onto dessert plates and chill until firm.

Halved plums or peaches
Thin sugar cookies

Serve cheese mixture as a spread for fruit and cookies.

GARDEN OF EDEN MELON

Cantaloupes, honeydews, Crenshaw, and other melons can begin a meal or provide a refreshing ending. Here, a tangy sauce enhances the sweet, subtle flavor of a honeydew.

PREPARATION TIME 5 MINUTES   SERVES 6 TO 8
CHILLING TIME 30 MINUTES

1   honeydew, cut in wedges
2   cups sliced or diced peaches
1   cup sliced strawberries
1   cup blueberries or raspberries

Be sure melon and other fruits are prime ripe and well chilled.

1   cup sour cream
1   tablespoon honey
½   teaspoon dry mustard
2   teaspoons lime juice

Stir sauce ingredients together and chill during dinner. When serving, top each wedge of melon with peaches and berries. Let each diner add the sauce topping.

THE "WHAT'S IT MADE OF?" PUDDING

When we made this pudding for the first time, we kept its main ingredient a secret. Even after our children raved about it, we hesitated to tell them. And with good reason. After all, a pudding made out of soybeans, *soybeans,* sounds like certain disaster. But oddly enough, this pudding isn't just good, it's great. High in protein. And delicious!

PREPARATION TIME 7 MINUTES   SERVES 6
BAKING TIME 55 MINUTES

  2   cups cooked soybeans, drained

In blender or food processor, transform soybeans into a smooth paste.

  ¼   teaspoon salt
  ½   teaspoon ginger
  1   teaspoon cinnamon
  2   eggs, beaten
  ¾   cup honey
  ¾   cup milk
  ¼   cup instant dry milk, dissolved in the ¾ cup milk

Thoroughly mix all these ingredients with the soybeans. Pour into an oiled 8-inch layer cake pan. Bake in a 350° oven for 55 minutes, or until set.

  ⅓ to ½ cup coarsely chopped walnuts

Five minutes before pudding is done, press nuts lightly over its surface. Return pan to oven for the final 5 minutes of baking. Serve warm or cold from the cake pan and topped with whipped cream or ice cream.

RIGHT AWAY RICE PUDDING

To say that this pudding is easy to prepare is an understatement. All you have to do, if you have cooked rice in the refrigerator—and you should have—is add a few ingredients. Aside from chilling the mixture, that's absolutely all that has to be done.

PREPARATION TIME 5 MINUTES   SERVES 6

> 3 cups cold cooked brown rice
> 1 cup raisins
> ¼ cup brown sugar (packed)
> 1 cup coarsely chopped walnuts
> 2 cups plain yogurt
>   Sprinkling of cinnamon
> 2 teaspoons lemon juice

Mix. Chill. Serve.

INDIAN PUDDING

American Indians in colonial times were great corn planters. Therefore they had to devise all sorts of recipes with corn as a basic
ingredient. Since they weren't a time-conscious people, they
thought nothing of spending a few hours on a pudding. This pudding, containing all the Indian's traditional ingredients, has been
speeded up for the sake of the modern consumer

PREPARATION TIME 5 MINUTES   SERVES 4
COOKING TIME 7 MINUTES

> ½ cup cornmeal
> ¼ cup whole wheat flour
> 3 cups cold water

Mix cornmeal and flour together in a saucepan. Stir in the cold
water. Bring to a boil, then simmer until the cornmeal has become
soft and thick.

> 2 tablespoons oil
> ⅓ cup honey
> ½ teaspoon salt
> ¼ teaspoon cloves
> ⅛ teaspoon ginger

Stir all these ingredients into the cornmeal mixture. Serve hot or
cold with cream.

OLÉ GRANOLA ROLL

This dessert is especially easy to prepare if you have commercial peanut butter and granola on hand. It's still easy—and perhaps better—if you make them yourself. You're then positive the peanut butter doesn't contain mono- and diglycerides—whatever they are. In a blender or food processor, peanuts can be transformed into peanut butter in hardly any time at all. (The blender requires that a little oil be added.) As for granola, the recipe we use merely requires mixing together 3 cups rolled oats, 1 cup wheat germ, 1 cup sesame seeds, ¼ cup oil, ¾ cup honey, 1 teaspoon vanilla, dash of salt. You then spread this mixture fairly evenly on cookie sheets and bake it at 325°, until it's turned a golden brown. Stir occasionally, for the edges brown first.

To make an Olé Granola Roll:

PREPARATION TIME 5 MINUTES   **SERVES 4**

    ½   **cup peanut butter**
    ½   **cup granola**

Blend these two ingredients.

    ½   **cup raisins**

Work the raisins into the mixture and form a log that's about an inch in diameter. Chill. (This can be speeded up by putting the log in your freezer for 5 to 10 minutes before refrigerating it.) Slice when ready to serve. If you prefer, the mixture can be made into shapes other than a roll—a ball, for example, golf ball size. Rolled in shredded coconut, they look quite pretty.

BOURBON STREET BARS

These faintly boozy little cakes are deliciously appealing, especially after a virtuous meal that's loaded with vitamins and trace elements. We tell ourselves that a little sin never hurt anybody, but just in case these bars conjure up visions of Fat Tuesday, we'd like to point out that the only *butter* in them is used for greasing the pan.

PREPARATION TIME 10 MINUTES   MAKES 16 2-INCH BARS
BAKING TIME 25 MINUTES

- ¾   cup brown sugar, firmly packed
- 1   teaspoon cinnamon
- ¼   teaspoon salt
- 2   1-ounce squares unsweetened chocolate, ground or grated
- ½   teaspoon baking powder
- 1   cup all-purpose flour

In a large bowl, combine above ingredients.

- 2   eggs
- 2   tablespoons bourbon, or 1 teaspoon vanilla extract, if you prefer
- 2   tablespoons honey

Add eggs, bourbon, and honey to the flour mixture and beat until well mixed.

- 1   cup coarsely chopped walnuts

Stir in the nuts. Spread the mixture in a well-greased 8-x-8-inch baking pan and bake in a 325° oven for 20 to 25 minutes, or until top is firm when touched lightly. Cool on a rack and cut into squares.

QUICKER APPLE STRUDEL

We remember how Grandmother used to make strudel. She'd mix up the dough and knead it mercilessly, sometimes slamming it down on the counter with a resounding whack. Then she'd let it "rest" while she prepared the apple filling. The fun part came when she covered the big round oak table with a clean white tablecloth, rolled out the dough into a big circle and then, slipping her hands under the dough palms down, she'd pull and stretch it until the edges were hanging over the table and the dough was so thin you could "read a newspaper through it."

Someday, we'll probably try to make strudel Grandmother's way, but for now we rely on ready-made phyllo, the thin Greek pastry leaves available in many gourmet shops and ethnic grocery stores. We do use Grandmother's filling, but we shred the apples, rather than slicing them as she did, because they bake faster that way. See page 37 for information on handling phyllo.

PREPARATION TIME 25 MINUTES   **MAKES 1 STRUDEL ROLL**
BAKING TIME 15 TO 20 MINUTES

> 1½ pounds tart cooking apples, peeled, cored, and shredded on a coarse grater
> ¾ teaspoon cinnamon
> ⅓ cup raisins
> ½ cup chopped pecans or walnuts

Toss apples with other ingredients and set aside.

> ¼ pound phyllo leaves
> ¼ pound butter, melted

Remove ¼ of the leaves from a 1-pound package of phyllo and lay them in a stack on a lightly dampened cloth. Return the rest of the leaves to their package, seal tightly and refrigerate. Spread a second dampened cloth and on it, one at a time, stack the leaves with the long end toward you, brushing each one with melted butter as you stack them. (Don't try to cover each entire leaf with butter—just several broad swipes up and down or across will be enough.) Brush the top leaf very generously with butter. When you have buttered the whole stack of leaves, it's time to add the filling.

⅔ **cup brown sugar**
butter
cinnamon

Add the sugar to the apple mixture, mixing lightly, and spoon it in a band along the long edge of the stack, about 2 inches from the edge, and 2 inches from each side. Drizzle with melted butter. Using the cloth as an aid, roll the filling up loosely, as in making a jelly roll. After filling has been completely wrapped around one time, turn in the edges and continue rolling until you come to the end of the dough. Carefully lift the strudel and place it, seam side down, on a well-buttered baking sheet. If it won't fit on the diagonal, bend it to a crescent shape. Brush top generously with butter and sprinkle with a little cinnamon. Bake at 425° for 25 minutes. If allowed to cool, reheat slightly before serving.

SOUR CREAM CAKE

This is an especially good cake for company. It's easy to make, light as one small feather, and has a luxurious appearance. If you're diet conscious, yogurt may be substituted for the sour cream.

PREPARATION TIME 15 MINUTES   SERVES 10 TO 12
BAKING TIME 55 MINUTES

> ¾   cup butter
> 1   cup brown sugar, firmly packed

Beat butter and sugar until thoroughly blended.

> 2   eggs, beaten
> 1   cup sour cream or yogurt
> 1   teaspoon vanilla extract

Add these ingredients to the butter-sugar mixture. Set aside.

> 1¾   cups unbleached white flour
> ¼   cup wheat germ
> 1   teaspoon baking powder
> ½   teaspoon baking soda

Mix thoroughly. Add gradually to the reserved mixture. Pour approximately half of the resulting batter into a greased 10-inch tube pan.

> ¾   cup chopped walnuts
> ¼   cup brown sugar
> 1   teaspoon cinnamon

Blend. Sprinkle half over the batter in pan. Pour in rest of batter and top with remaining nut mixture. Bake in 350° oven for 55 minutes.

DARK AND HANDSOME

Here's a cake, in pound cake form, with an irresistibly rich chocolatey flavor. We gild the lily by topping it with vanilla ice cream or whipped cream. Either actually enhances the cake's already superb taste.

PREPARATION TIME 10 MINUTES   SERVES 8
BAKING TIME 40 TO 45 MINUTES

 1   1-ounce square unsweetened chocolate
 1   tablespoon butter

Put chocolate and butter in Pyrex measuring cup, place on *low* heat.

 1   cup flour
 1   cup sugar
 1   teaspoon baking powder
     Pinch salt

Sift dry ingredients together. Set oven at 350°.

 1   egg
 ¾   cup milk (approximately)

Put egg in Pyrex cup containing melted butter and chocolate. Pour in milk until it measures one cup. Add to dry ingredients and mix thoroughly. Pour into greased 8½-x-4½-x-2½-inch loaf pan. Bake until toothpick inserted in center comes out clean, approximately 40 to 45 minutes.

CHEESELESS CHEESECAKE

Naturally, the paradoxical aspect of this cake adds to its interest. An endless, futile discussion can be held as to what makes it taste like cheese. Some will say it's the sour cream that does it; others will agree, but add that the lemon peel is not an inconsequential factor. Meanwhile, the cake will disappear—be ravenously consumed, that is.

Prepare a graham cracker crust for an 8-inch pie pan. Make crumbs of 15 graham crackers. Combine ¼ cup butter and ¼ cup sugar with crackers. Do this by hand, or more easily, in a blender or food processor. Press prepared crumbs into pie pan. Put crust in refrigerator.

PREPARATION TIME FOR CAKE FILLING 5 MINUTES
COOKING TIME 1 MINUTE   SERVES 6

- 1 cup milk
- 2 tablespoons cornstarch
- ⅓ cup sugar
  Few thin strips lemon peel, cut from lemon with swivel peeler

Blend in blender. Pour into a heavy saucepan, bring to a boil, stirring constantly, and boil for 1 minute. Remove from heat.

- 1 teaspoon vanilla extract
- 1 cup sour cream

Add to the milk mixture and stir thoroughly. Take crust from the refrigerator and spoon this mixture into it. Chill until cake's ready to be served.
Note: If you wish to cut down on calories, substitute yogurt for half the sour cream.

HIDDEN TREASURE CAKE

The treasure is golden grated carrot. The carrot is not really detectable as a vegetable, but helps make the cake moist and delicious. You can put your own stamp on this cake by adding your favorite spices, such as nutmeg, cloves, or ginger. Raisins, chopped prunes, or currants are also good additions. If you want to cut down on the baking time, bake in two 8-inch cake pans for 35 minutes.

PREPARATION TIME 10 MINUTES   SERVES 10 TO 12
BAKING TIME 60 MINUTES

- 1¾ cups brown sugar
- 2 cups flour
- 2 teaspoons baking soda
- 1 teaspoon salt
- 1 teaspoon cinnamon

Mix ingredients together in a large bowl.

- 1 cup vegetable oil
- 4 eggs
- 3 cups grated carrot
- 1 teaspoon vanilla extract
- 1 cup nuts, coarsely chopped
- 2 teaspoons grated orange peel (optional)

Add oil and mix well. Beat in eggs, one at a time. Stir in grated carrot, vanilla, nuts, and orange peel, if used.

Pour batter into a greased and flour-dusted 10-inch tube pan or bundt pan. Bake at 350° about 1 hour, or until a toothpick inserted in center comes out clean. Cool in pan 15 minutes. Turn out on wire rack to cool thoroughly. If you wish, glaze cake with Lemon Glaze.

Note: Once, when making this cake, we were short of carrots and substituted grated zucchini for 1 cup of the carrots. The result was a great success. "Hmmm," said one taster, spotting the tiny green flecks among the orange, "pistachio!" Another time we added ¼ cup cocoa, 1½ teaspoons baking powder, and 1 teaspoon cinnamon along with the dry ingredients and substituted zucchini for all of the carrots. The cake was rich and moist and the zucchini was completely masked.

LEMON GLAZE

1¼ cups confectioners' sugar
2 tablespoons lemon juice
4 tablespoons butter, melted

Stir ingredients together with a wire whisk (or mix in a blender or food processor) until smooth. Pour glaze over top of cake and allow it to dribble down over the sides.

CHEESECAKE SUPERSTAR

If we had this cake often, we'd end up looking like Babar and Celeste. But once in a while, after an unreasonably austere meal, let's indulge! This recipe requires a food processor or blender. If a blender is used, divide the ingredients in half and process in two batches.

PREPARATION TIME 10 MINUTES   MAKES ONE 8-INCH CAKE
BAKING TIME 40 MINUTES
CHILLING TIME SEVERAL HOURS OR OVERNIGHT

Preheat oven to 375°.

10 almonds, or cashews
12 graham cracker squares
¼ cup (½ stick) butter, cut in pieces

Place nuts and graham crackers in container of food processor or blender and blend until pulverized. Add butter and blend again for 2 or 3 seconds. Reserve ¼ cup of the mixture for use as a topping.

Press remaining crumb mixture into bottom and part way up the sides of a buttered 8-inch springform cake pan. Set in refrigerator while making cake.

1 scant cup sugar
Strip of lemon peel (no white part)
3 eggs
Pinch of salt

Place sugar and lemon peel in food processor. Process for a few seconds until well blended. Add eggs and salt, process again.

2 8-ounce packages cream cheese, broken into chunks

With motor running, drop pieces of cream cheese into egg mixture and process 15 seconds.

3 cups sour cream
1 teaspoon vanilla extract
⅛ teaspoon cinnamon
⅛ teaspoon nutmeg

Add ingredients to cheese mixture and blend 10 seconds until mixture is smooth and batter bubbles up when you stop the motor. Pour into prepared pan. Sprinkle reserved crumbs on top of cake, mainly on the outer edge with a few in the center. Bake at 375° for 40 minutes. Allow to cool for one hour, then refrigerate.

SPIRAL SOUFFLÉ CAKE

This beautiful cake is so easy to make that the compliments it always elicits are almost embarrassing. Although it looks wickedly rich and fattening, there's no butter or flour in the cake itself, just flavored whipped cream in the filling. A wonderful party dessert, it can be made well ahead and refrigerated, or frozen if you like. We sometimes make it for birthdays.

PREPARATION TIME 20 MINUTES   **MAKES ONE 15-INCH ROLL**
BAKING TIME 30 MINUTES

Preheat oven to 350°

Cover the bottom of a 10-x-15-inch jelly roll pan with a piece of aluminum foil 10 inches wide and about 20 inches long, allowing the excess length to hang over each end of the pan. Butter the foil and the sides of the pan well. Sprinkle pan with flour, knocking out the excess. Assemble all ingredients and have them at hand.

> 7   **egg whites at room temperature**
> Scant ½ **teaspoon cream of tartar**

Place egg whites in large bowl of an electric mixer and beat until foamy. Add cream of tartar and beat until very stiff, shiny peaks form when beater is lifted. With a rubber spatula, gently scoop the beaten egg whites into a large bowl, taking care not to deflate them.

> 7   **egg yolks at room temperature**
> ½   **cup sugar**
> 3   **tablespoons cocoa**
> 1   **teaspoon vanilla extract**
> ¾   **cup ground walnuts or almonds**

Without washing the bowl or beater, place egg yolks in the mixer bowl and beat vigorously until they become thick and lighter in color. Beat in remaining ingredients, mixing well. With a rubber spatula, gently start folding the yolk mixture into the whites. As you fold, add the nuts, a small handful at a time. Don't overblend!

Pour mixture into the prepared pan, spread it gently, but evenly, to all sides and corners of the pan. Place it in 350° oven and bake until surface rebounds when gently touched, about 30 minutes.

Remove cake from oven, cover with damp cloth and set it, still in the pan, on a rack until cool. Cake will deflate as it cools.

confectioners' sugar

Remove cloth and dust top of cake lightly with confectioners' sugar. Lift cake from pan by means of the overhanging ends of foil and invert it onto a large piece of waxed paper. Peel off aluminum foil adhering to the cake.

1   cup well-chilled heavy cream
1   teaspoon light corn syrup
3   tablespoons chocolate or coffee-flavored liqueur

Whip cream and corn syrup in a small bowl. As cream begins to thicken, add liqueur. When cream is of spreading consistency, spread it evenly over the cake, and beginning with a long end, roll cake up like a jelly roll. Chill, seam side down, until serving time, or freeze. Cut in slices to serve If frozen, allow to thaw slightly before cutting.

Variation: To make a nonchocolate version of this cake, omit the cocoa and reduce the sugar to 6 tablespoons. Fill the roll with whipped cream that has been comoıned with chopped or puréed fruit, such as strawberries.

QUICK VANILLA ICE CREAM

Wholesome, delicious, easily and quickly made. Nothing, of course, is perfect. See note below.

PREPARATION TIME 7 MINUTES   SERVES 4 TO 6
FREEZING TIME 1½ HOURS, AT FREEZER'S COLDEST SETTING

 2   eggs
 ¾   cup sugar

Beat eggs in electric mixer, or by hand, until foamy. Add sugar gradually to the eggs, beating until thickened.

 1   cup milk
 1   pint (2 cups) whipping cream
 2½ teaspoons vanilla extract
 ⅛   teaspoon salt

Mix thoroughly into egg-sugar mixture. Pour into two ice-cube trays and freeze. Remove cubes of ice cream as needed. Fine as topping for pie, cake, and chocolate pudding.

Note: The bottom of each cube, you'll find, will be somewhat crystalline. If this bothers you, whip the ice cream in blender or food processor until the crystals are broken up and the ice cream is completely smooth.

BANANA ICE CREAM PIE

A handsome, rich dessert. Because it appears far more complex and expensive than it is, it's a good one for company—especially company you want to impress. Prepare the pie early; then the time needed for freezing can't possibly be a problem.

PREPARATION TIME 7 MINUTES   **SERVES 6**
FREEZING TIME 1 HOUR

Put electric mixer bowl and beater in freezer. Set freezer at coldest temperature.

2   eggs
½   cup honey
1   teaspoon vanilla extract

Beat eggs. Mix them thoroughly with honey and vanilla.

1   pint (2 cups) whipping cream

Put cream in the chilled bowl and whip until fairly stiff. Fold into egg mixture. Clean bowl and beater and return to freezer.

1   ripe banana

Mash banana with a potato masher. Continue folding the whipped cream, blending the mashed banana into the cream and the other ingredients. Pour into 10-inch pie pan. Place pan in freezer. After a half hour, or when filling has frozen about two inches from the edge of the pan, put the filling into chilled mixer bowl and beat until smooth. Return the filling to the pie pan and put the pan back in the freezer. When the filling has solidified, remove pan from freezer. Decorate the surface of the pie with banana slices. Cut into wedges to serve.

CHOCOLATE MOUSSE

If you keep a supply of this silken smooth mousse in the freezer for special occasions, you'll probably find yourself inventing "special occasions." It's rich, dark, and outrageously good.

PREPARATION TIME 7 MINUTES　　　　　　　　　　**SERVES ABOUT 15**
FREEZING TIME 2 HOURS

> **4　1-ounce squares unsweetened chocolate**
> **1　cup butter or margarine**

Melt butter and chocolate together over low heat, taking care not to scorch them. Pour mixture into food processor or blender.

> **1¾ cups confectioners' sugar**

With motor running, add sugar gradually to chocolate mixture, mixing until well blended. Scrape down sides as needed.

> **4　eggs**
> **2　tablespoons Cognac**

Add eggs and Cognac and blend until fluffy. Spoon mixture into individual muffin-size cups.

> **½　cup toasted chopped almonds**

Sprinkle nuts evenly over mousse. Freeze until firm.

NIFTY NUT CRUST

Pecans give this tender, crisp piecrust an unusually fine flavor. There's no cholesterol present, and the crust is made right in the pie pan—no rolling!

PREPARATION TIME 5 MINUTES   **MAKES ONE 1-CRUST PIE**
BAKING TIME (FOR PREBAKED SHELL) 15 TO 18 MINUTES

Preheat oven to 400°.

> 1½ **cups flour**
> 1   **teaspoon salt**
> 1½ **teaspoons sugar**

Sift ingredients directly into the pie pan.

> ½   **cup finely chopped or ground pecans**

Stir pecans into flour mixture with a fork until well blended.

> 6   **tablespoons polyunsaturated oil**
> 3   **tablespoons water**

Mix oil and water together in a small measuring cup, and gradually pour into the dry ingredients, stirring with a fork as you pour. After moisture has all been absorbed by the flour mixture, continue stirring with the fork until well mixed. If dough is too soft to handle, chill a few minutes in the freezer to make working with it easier. With your fingers, press pastry into the bottom and around the sides of the pan, making it as thin and even as possible. Bake immediately, or refrigerate for later use.

If crust is to be used as a prebaked shell, prick bottom and sides of pastry well with a fork, place a sheet of foil on the crust and lightly mold it to the shape of the crust. Fill the foil with dried beans and bake crust in a 400° oven for 5 minutes. Reduce heat to 375° and continue baking 10 to 15 minutes longer.

WHEAT GERM PIECRUST

Here's a variation of Nifty Nut Crust, and it includes a top crust. The wheat germ adds interesting texture as well as flavor.

PREPARATION TIME 10 MINUTES   MAKES ONE 9-INCH DOUBLE CRUST

- **2** **cups unbleached white flour**
- **1** **teaspoon salt**
- **2** **teaspoons sugar**

Sift ingredients into a bowl.

- **½** **cup toasted wheat germ**
- **½** **cup ground nuts**
- **1** **teaspoon grated lemon peel**

Stir ingredients into the flour mixture until well blended.

- **½** **cup polyunsaturated oil**
- **6** **tablespoons water**

Pour oil and water into a small measuring cup and add gradually to dry ingredients while stirring with a fork until well mixed. Gather the dough into two balls, one slightly larger than the other. Pat the smaller ball into a flat circle, wrap it in waxed paper, and place in the refrigerator. Press the larger ball of dough into the bottom and sides of a 9-inch pie pan and refrigerate it while you prepare the desired filling. When ready to fill the pie, remove the flat circle of dough from the refrigerator and place it between two 12-inch squares of waxed paper. Place the squares on a dampened counter and roll the dough into a 12-inch circle. Peel off the top sheet of paper. After filling the bottom crust, lift the dough on the waxed paper and place it, paper side up, over the filling. Peel off the remaining paper. Seal edges of crusts, trim off excess dough. Pierce top crust with a fork to allow steam to escape. Bake.

Note: If you wish to make a single, prebaked shell, follow directions for Nifty Nut Crust, substituting wheat germ for half the nuts and adding ½ teaspoon lemon peel.

SPINACH DESSERT NIÇOISE

We'll admit that spinach in a dessert sounds odd, and we can't help wondering how this pie came into being. We have been told that this interesting variation on apple pie is a beloved dessert in the south of France. Try it. We think you'll be pleasantly astonished.

PREPARATION TIME 15 MINUTES   SERVES 8
BAKING TIME 30 MINUTES

Preheat oven to 375°.

6   **medium-sized cooking apples**

Peel and core apples, slice them thinly, then cut slices into pieces.

¼   **cup raisins**
3   **tablespoons dark rum**

Combine raisins and rum and boil for 2 or 3 minutes. Set aside.

1   **10-ounce package frozen chopped spinach, cooked, and all excess moisture removed**
¼   **cup chopped walnuts**
½   **cup brown sugar**
¼   **pound Jack cheese, shredded**
2   **eggs, beaten**

Combine these ingredients. Stir in the rum-soaked raisins, drained if necessary.

1   **unbaked double piecrust (we suggest Wheat Germ Piecrust)**
2   **tablespoons apricot jam**

Spread jam on bottom crust. Pour in filling, distributing it evenly over jam. Cover filling with the top crust, sealing edges. Cut air vents in top crust. Bake 30 minutes or until apples are tender.

Sugar
Cinnamon

Remove pie from oven and sprinkle with a little sugar and cinnamon while still hot.

RICH CHOCOLATE PUDDING MIX

This pudding deserves to be described as rich—and rich in a good sense; the recipe somehow transmutes its simple ingredients into an opulent chocolate. Because the pudding's so good, having the convenience of a mix for it makes it all the more appealing.

PREPARATION TIME 10 MINUTES   **SERVES 20**

    4   1-quart packages instant dry milk
    1   cup sugar
    ½   cup cornstarch
    1¼   cups cocoa
    1   teaspoon salt

Blend thoroughly. (Done most easily in electric mixer or food processor.) Store in a large, tightly covered jar.

RICH CHOCOLATE PUDDING

PREPARATION TIME 5 MINUTES   **SERVES 4**
COOKING TIME 3 MINUTES

    1   cup milk
    1   cup water
    ¾   cup Rich Chocolate Pudding Mix

In a heavy saucepan, put milk and ½ cup of the water. Heat to simmering. Thoroughly blend the pudding mix with the remaining ½ cup of water, then stir it slowly into the milk-water mixture. Bring to a boil, stirring all the while to prevent sticking and burning. Boil for one minute.

    1   teaspoon vanilla extract

Stir into pudding. Cool by putting saucepan in a large bowl of cold water. Chill. To speed chilling time, put saucepan in freezer for 10 minutes or so.

OMNI OATMEAL MIX

Go on, steal an idea from manufacturers. They make baking mixes, so why can't you? Here's one you can throw together quickly and use to make many good-tasting things. We include five possible recipes. We call it "omni" because it's an everything mix.

PREPARATION TIME 5 MINUTES   **MAKES 8 CUPS**

- 4 cups oatmeal
- 2 cups whole wheat flour
- 2 cups unbleached white flour
- 3 tablespoons baking powder
- 1 teaspoon salt

Place all ingredients in a large bowl and blend well with a wire whisk (or mix on low speed in an electric mixer). Store in an airtight container in a cool, dry place. Always stir or shake the mix well before using.

ORANGE OATMEAL MUFFINS

PREPARATION TIME 5 MINUTES   **MAKES 12 MUFFINS**
BAKING TIME 15 TO 18 MINUTES

Preheat oven to 425°.

- 2 eggs
- 3 tablespoons brown sugar
- ⅔ cup milk
- ¼ cup (½ stick) butter or margarine
  Thin rind of half an orange (remove with swivel peeler)
- ½ cup raisins

Place ingredients in blender or food processor and blend until raisins are coarsely cut.

2¼ cups Omni Oatmeal Mix

Pour mix into a large bowl. Add blended egg mixture and stir with a fork just enough to moisten ingredients. Spoon into greased muffin cups and bake at 425° for 15 to 18 minutes.

CHOCOLATE CHIP COOKIES

PREPARATION TIME 7 MINUTES   MAKES ABOUT 3 DOZEN COOKIES
BAKING TIME 10 TO 12 MINUTES

Preheat oven to 375°.

> ½   cup butter or other shortening
> ½   cup brown sugar

Cream butter and sugar until light and fluffy.

> 1   egg
> 1   teaspoon vanilla extract

Add egg and vanilla and beat well.

> 2   cups Omni Oatmeal Mix

Stir in mix and beat until smooth.

> ½   cup coarsely chopped nuts
> 1   6-ounce package chocolate chips
> ½   cup shredded or flaked coconut

Stir in nuts, chocolate and coconut. Drop mixture by heaping tea-spoonfuls onto an ungreased baking sheet. Bake at 375° for 10 to 12 minutes.

Note: To make these cookies in *less* time using a food processor: Cream shortening and sugar in container until smooth. Add egg and vanilla and turn on and off 6 times or until ingredients are well blended. Add mix and turn machine on and off about 8 times. Stir in remaining ingredients by hand.

CHEESECAKE MINIATURES

PREPARATION TIME 10 MINUTES   **MAKES 16 BARS**
BAKING TIME 35 TO 40 MINUTES

Preheat oven to 350°.

- ⅓ cup butter or margarine
- ⅓ cup brown sugar
- 1 cup Omni Oatmeal Mix

Blend ingredients together with fingers until crumbly.

- ½ cup chopped walnuts or other nuts, or toasted sunflower seeds

Add nuts to the mixture. Remove ½ cup and reserve for topping. Press remainder into a greased, 8-inch square baking pan and bake at 350° for 12 to 15 minutes.

- 8 ounces cream cheese, softened
- 1 egg
- 2 tablespoons milk
- 3 tablespoons frozen lemonade concentrate
- 1 tablespoon honey
- ½ teaspoon vanilla extract
- ¼ teaspoon nutmeg

Place ingredients in food processor or blender and mix until smooth. Spread over baked crust and sprinkle with reserved oatmeal mixture. Bake at 350° for 25 minutes. Cool and cut into 2-inch squares. If made ahead, refrigerate.

PEACH DELIGHT

This is a variation of Cheesecake Miniatures.

PREPARATION TIME 10 MINUTES   MAKES ONE 9-INCH PIE
BAKING TIME 37 MINUTES

Preneat oven to 350°.

> 1½   cups Omni Oatmeal Mix
> ¾   cup butter
> ⅓   cup brown sugar
> ½   cup coarsely chopped walnuts

Cut butter into mix, add sugar and blend with fingers until crumbly. Mix in nuts. Set aside ½ cup of the mixture for topping. Press remainder into bottom and sides of a buttered 9-inch pie pan. Bake at 350° for 12 minutes. Set aside to cool.

> 6   ounces cream cheese
> 3   tablespoons honey
> 1   egg
> 1   tablespoon milk
> 1   tablespoon lemon juice
>   Grated rind of one lemon
> ¼   teaspoon vanilla extract
> ½   teaspoon cinnamon

In large bowl of mixer, beat cream cheese to soften and blend in honey. Add remaining ingredients and beat to mix well. (Or, place all ingredients in container of food processor and process.) Pour mixture in prebaked crust.

> **3 to 4 fresh peaches, peeled and sliced**

Arrange peach slices over the filling and sprinkle the reserved topping evenly over the top. Bake at 350° for 25 minutes. Cool thoroughly and cut in small wedges to serve. If made ahead, refrigerate.

ORANGE OATMEAL PANCAKES

PREPARATION TIME 3 MINUTES   **MAKES 12 SMALL PANCAKES**
BAKING TIME 10 MINUTES

Preheat griddle to medium hot.

- **1** cup orange juice
- **2** tablespoons milk
- **3** tablespoons butter
- **2** eggs
- **3** tablespoons honey
- **1½** cups Omni Oatmeal Mix

Place all ingredients in blender or food processor and blend until smooth, scraping down once or twice. Pour onto hot, greased griddle, ¼ cup at a time, and bake until browned on both sides. Serve with sliced strawberries and/or bananas and yogurt.

Entertaining the Easy Way

According to one authority on entertaining, the most important duty of the successful host is to "create the illusion that you are having as good a time as everybody else." Well, we'd like to say right here that illusions aren't enough for us. If we can't have the real thing, we'd do better to forgo entertaining altogether. In fact, we've heard several accomplished hosts, practitioners of the old-style elegant dinner party, say that they're tired of the whole business and *are* going to give it up. They will, they say, devise other ways of seeing their friends. Dinner parties are just too much work!

In our minds, though, food and friendship are synergistic, and we'd really hate to give up the tribal ritual of preparing a special meal for our friends on our own turf. So we've taken to using certain tricks, techniques, and corner-cutters to minimize the work. We'd like to say *eliminate* the work, but we still have hang-ups about honesty.

Our most popular ploy is a variation of the old-fashioned, church basement bit of nostalgia called a "potluck" or "covered dish" supper, to which everyone contributed a dish to be shared by all. As we recall from our dim Midwestern memories, there was a staggering abundance of good food at those dinners, but usually a hodge-podge of food that didn't really go well together. That shortcoming mattered less to us then than it would now.

Usually, our practice is to supply the main dish and then to consult with our friends as to what "go with" they would like to bring. We can remember one wonderfully delightful occasion, though, when the guests brought *all* the food and we merely supplied the setting—put out the company towels, checked the goblets for fingerprints, and turned on the ambience. It was a splendid feast, and we felt like the ultimate liberated host. We knew we had found "a better way."

The advantages of cooperative cooking are obvious: No one person has to do all the work. Each contributor can bring a specialty—a dish he or she really enjoys making and does superlatively well. The slight edge of competition that's bound to occur, spurs each to greater heights, and the result is a Lucullan banquet that bears little resemblance to the steamy, fragrant, church suppers of our youth.

Another of our favorite approaches to entertaining is an idea we borrowed from restaurants we've visited across the country, the Salad Bar. All the elements of several types of salad are arranged on trays or in bowls, and each guest can choose favorites and come away with a personal expression of what a good salad should be. These events can become hilarious, with each person vying to achieve the ultimate salad. With plenty of substantial selections, such as marinated beans and other vegetables, hard-cooked eggs, and cheeses included in the display, it's not at all difficult to construct a completely satisfying and delicious meal. The offerings can be as numerous and as elaborate as you wish. All the choices, being cold, can be prepared ahead of time and refrigerated.

Sometimes we make it a Soup and Salad Bar and include several hearty soups (all prepared well ahead and reheated), served in attractive tureens.

Another variation is the Sandwich Buffet. Several kinds of crusty bread and rolls, and a collection of possible fillings, allow each guest to unleash creative urges and put together something totally mind boggling. Add a group of garnishes and perhaps a platter of sprouts, and everyone becomes a Dagwood Bumstead! Pocket bread, or pita, is particularly good for this type of luncheon. It holds the filling neatly—a definite advantage.

Alternately, there might be the Soup and Sandwich Party or the Sandwich and Salad Luncheon.

This leads us to the surprising and pleasing meal that consists of nothing but Appetizers. Not a new idea—the Greeks have long had their *mézé*, the Italians their *antipasto*, the Danes their *smørrebrød*, the Russians their *zakuski* . . . It's fun, occasionally, just to nibble our way through the evening. If attention is paid to the variety, quantity, and quality of appetizers presented, it's a stimulating change from the expected and routine way of dining.

Another artful dodge is the Picnic Party. We rely on this one when we haven't the time or inclination to get the house in shelter magazine order. The party can be held on the beach, on a boat (if you—or they—happen to own one) or in some untrafficked park or woodland spot. On occasion, we schedule this picnic to precede a concert or theater performance when it becomes a Picnic for Patrons of the Arts. We bring the food—but never decline if our guests offer to help. We try to make the picnic menu a stopper—food that is more elegant than common picnic fare, but that transports well. A bottle of good wine or champagne, well chilled, doesn't hurt either.

Then there's the Dessert Party, when friends are invited to come after dinner for dessert. We try to have one, two, or sometimes three really special desserts. We usually give this one after we've squirreled away several desserts in the freezer over a period of time, so there's nothing to do but bring them out when the time comes.

There are occasions, of course, when nothing will do but a dinner party of elegance and substance. We seldom, if ever, have the formal sit-down variety—we think we'd need plenty of hired help to pull off such a show, and although time may be more precious than money, sometimes they're both in short supply! We do often have a Sit-down Buffet at which each guest helps himself and then finds a prearranged seat at a preset table.

Not believing in the overwork ethic, we've set up certain methods of operation designed to keep us out of the rest home and allow us to have as much fun as everyone else. Here are some things we subconsciously tell ourselves:

1. Choose dishes that can be completely cooked in advance and frozen, or can be prepared ahead, refrigerated, and then reheated. Try to include some cold dishes.

2. Select dishes that don't deteriorate if they can't be served immediately.

3. Have at least one very special, impressively attractive dish it can be a main course or a dessert—because how food looks is just as important as how it tastes, and it's certainly true that we often "eat with our eyes." Pay special attention to handsome serving utensils and garnishes; they can make all the difference. If you're inexperienced at garnishing, make a habit of collecting attractive food photos from magazines to inspire you.

4. After deciding on the menu, assemble the recipes and write out a shopping list. Plan your shopping time to coincide as closely as possible to preparation time so fruits, vegetables, and other foods will be at their peak when you use them.

5. Prepare as much of the food as possible in advance. Try to leave only the salad and reheating of other dishes for the day of the

party. If you plan to have a molded or marinated salad, even that can be done the day before.

6. Don't attempt major cleaning at the last minute. Do a thorough job several days before, and then give the house minor touchups each day to keep things in order.

7. Set the table and arrange the decorations the night before, if possible. Make a collection of interesting and dramatic objects to use in imaginative ways for centerpieces or coverings on a buffet table. They need not be rare or expensive. (Junk shops often yield great treasures at low cost.) Use what is at hand—a blanket of fresh green fern fronds can make an exotic, disposable table covering for a summer buffet. Try to get away from the old candles-and-flowers routine. Spend some time, when time is cheap, arranging your decorative objects in interesting ways, and you'll hardly have to think about how to do it when party time arrives.

8. If you're serving drinks, have them premixed and ready for the ice. Have limes and oranges sliced, lemon peel pared, coasters at the ready. Wine is easier to serve than mixed drinks, so don't discourage this preference. Be sure to have nonalcoholic beverages for those who request them. If you can, chill glasses.

9. If you have a *compañero* (spouse, roommate, paramour, etc.), work out a shared serving and clearing away system, with a clear definition of who's to do what and when.

10. If the party is large, minimize the later cleanup with disposable goblets, dishes, napkins, and tablecloths. There are attractive ones available. Arrange for their neat, unobtrusive disposal between courses and at the end of the meal. One way is to have a helper circulate with a large, white plastic bag.

11. Small children love parties, and when allowed to participate, often display great poise and decorum until the stimulation of the party atmosphere affects their young adrenals. Delinquency then ensues. As preventive medicine, you can: (a) Have them fed and tucked away before the party begins (often difficult to accomplish and keep accomplished). (b) Have a competent baby-sitter look after them during the party. (The sitter can trot them out for a brief, charming appearance.) Or (c) Deposit them at the home of a playmate for the night. (You can probably make a reciprocal deal.)

12. Older children can be something else. Depending on age and motivation, they can help, enjoy it, and gain experience. They can park cars, answer the door and telephone, take wraps, help prepare and serve food, and even clean up afterward.

13. Pets, which are effusive in their display of friendliness, should be kept restrained. They might scratch that new Lincoln Continental.

14. Post a menu where you can check it at serving time. You won't then find something in the refrigerator the next day that you forgot to serve.

15. Unless you live in the Mojave, have an alternate spot ready if your party is to be alfresco. Whenever our garden is very dry, we plan to serve outdoors. There's nothing like it to break the drought.

You may be wondering if we entertain only vegetarians. In our present circle of friends, the vegetarians are greatly outnumbered. But we never feel we must add meat to the menu to keep them happy. We've discovered that the nonvegetarians find the experience of vegetarian dishes novel, interesting, and satisfying, if not delicious. They often seem surprised and delighted that they've gotten through a whole meal with no trace of meat and haven't really missed it. And, besides, they haven't come just for the food, you know. They've come to spend time with us in our home, because they are our friends.

Helpful Hints

(To improve a dish and/or speed its preparation)

★ If you've kept whole wheat flour in the refrigerator, here's a quick way to warm it for breadmaking. Put the cold flour in a large skillet over medium heat, work fingers of both hands through the flour as it heats. When you feel the flour begin to warm, remove skillet from heat. Continue to work your fingers through the flour, however, until it's uniformly warm. This whole process takes only minutes, but it's necessary because cold flour retards yeast action.

★ Before freezing freshly baked bread, cool the bread. Then freeze it unwrapped. When frozen, wrap airtight in foil or freezer wrap. The reason: Center of bread may still be warm although outside feels cool to touch. If wrapped while warm, moisture may form and cause sogginess.

★ To cut freshly made bread more easily, use an electric knife.

★ If you want to prepare a casserole ahead of time, bake it for all but 20 minutes of the baking time. Cool. Then cover and keep in the refrigerator until 30 minutes before it's to be served. At that time put it in a preheated oven. In 10 minutes, the chilled casserole will be warm. The next 20 minutes will complete the baking.

★ Freshly baked bread will come out of a bread pan more easily if the pan has been greased with butter rather than with oil.

★ Cheese tastes best at room temperature. Remove from the refrigerator 30 to 60 minutes before use to allow it to warm. Exceptions: cottage cheese and cream cheese are best when removed from the refrigerator just before serving.

★ Heavy thread or thin wire are best for slicing crumbly cheeses like Gorgonzola or Stilton.

★ To shred soft cheese, cut in a few pieces and place in freezer until very cold.

★ When cooking cheese, keep at very low temperature, or add cheese during the last few minutes to prevent it from becoming tough or stringy.

★ Grated cheese topping on many dishes doesn't require cooking. The heat from both food and dish are enough to bring it to its best serving temperature.

★ If you have ends or assorted small pieces of cheese which have hardened, grate them together and use for toppings. This makes for interesting flavor combinations.

★ Before grating cheese, brush a little oil on the grater with a pastry brush; this will make washing the grater easier.

★ A little salt will bring out the flavor in chocolate.

★ To cream butter and sugar faster, rinse the bowl just before you do the creaming in very hot water.

★ When grating cheese in a blender for a recipe that also calls for bread crumbs, do them together. The crumbs will keep the cheese from sticking to the blender.

★ Mozzarella cheese can be cut easily, and into thin slices, with an electric knife.

★ For best results, don't whip too much cream at a time. The cream shouldn't be so deep that it covers the blades of the mixer.

★ A good way to see if the skillet is hot enough to fry eggs, or to cook French toast or grill sandwiches, is to sprinkle just a few drops of water on the buttered skillet. When the skillet's hot enough, the water will skitter around. If the water drops just sit, the skillet isn't hot enough. If the water evaporates immediately, the skillet is too hot.

★ This helpful hint is for those who admit they can boil water but can't boil an egg. First of all, an egg should be cooked, not boiled. Intense heat toughens the egg white. Therefore, to hard-cook eggs cover them with enough water to come at least an inch above the eggs and bring them just to the boiling point. Remove pan from heat, cover with lid and let stand in hot water 15 minutes for large eggs. Adjust time up or down for other sizes. Cool eggs immediately in cold water. Shells are then easier to remove, and dark surface on yolks is prevented.

★ To remove shell of a hard-cooked egg: Crackle shell by tapping gently all over. Roll egg between hands to loosen shell, then peel, starting at large end. Holding egg under running cold water or dipping in a bowl of water helps to ease off shell.

★ Should an egg crack while it's in hot water, lower flame and pour salt on the crack. This will prevent the egg white from escaping.

★ It's better to remove scrambled eggs from pan when they're slightly underdone; heat in eggs will complete cooking.

★ To peel garlic more easily, cut cloves in half and press their sides with a knife's handle or the flat of its blade. The peel should then come right off.

★ If honey is called for, always spread a film of oil on the measuring spoon or glass before the honey is poured into it. The honey will then pour out smoothly, and there'll be no waste.

★ To make wooden handles ovenproof, wrap them with foil.

★ Head lettuce stays greener longer if its core has been removed. Remove core by striking it against a hard surface. The core can then be pulled or twisted out.

★ Though red lentils are harder to find than brown, they unquestionablv cook much faster than the brown variety.

★ If you're out of lemons and need one, a lime can serve as a substitute.

★ Here's a skill that will save you time. Pour various dry measurements into your hand. When you do this, memorize how each measurement looks. Eventually, you should be able to get along occasionally without measuring spoons.

★ To peel an onion more easily, cut off ends, cut it in half and peel each half.

★ Arranging items in alphabetical order will definitely save you time. This applies to spices, if kept in racks or cubbyholes. Canned goods should at least be arranged by type. When you put something back, exercise great control and put it in the spot from which you took it.

★ Potatoes will bake faster if put in very hot water for 10 minutes and then dried before baking.

★ Should the fruit pie you're baking ooze juice and cause the oven to smoke, you can stop the smoking by scattering salt on the juice drippings.

★ Use an ice-cream scoop for putting batter in muffin tins. A scoop holds just the right amount. It's also handy in forming patties. All you do is take a scoop of whatever it is you're measuring, and pat down the mound that the scoop forms.

★ If you've put too much salt in something you're cooking, add raw potato slices. They'll absorb the salt. When the dish is done, discard them.

★ When you double a recipe, don't double the salt. Instead, use half again as much, then taste to see if it needs more.

★ A bit of sugar coaxes out the flavor of a tomato.

★ For the weight conscious: Use yogurt instead of oil or cream as a thickener. For salad dressing: to ¼ teaspoon Dijon mustard, salt, pepper, and 2 tablespoons wine vinegar, add 1 tablespoon oil and 3 tablespoons yogurt.

In making a piecrust, substitute cottage cheese for some of the fat (4 tablespoons butter and 4 tablespoons sieved cottage cheese to 1½ cups flour).

To convert cottage cheese into a low-calorie "sour cream": Put a pound of cottage cheese in a wire strainer, hold under running water until water runs clear, not milky. Drain thoroughly. Blend the drained cottage cheese with ¼ cup skimmed milk and 2 tablespoons lemon juice until smooth.

To convert cottage cheese into a low calorie "cream cheese": Put the cottage cheese in a food processor and process with steel knife until smooth. (A dry cottage cheese works better than creamed cottage cheese.)

Index